FROM THE MUD TO THE MIRE

JOHN (JACK) HARNEY

AuthorHouse™ LLC
1663 Liberty Drive
Bloomington, IN 47403
www.authorhouse.com
Phone: 1-800-839-8640

Published by AuthorHouse   08/25/2014

ISBN: 978-1-4969-2098-0 (sc)
ISBN: 978-1-4969-2099-7 (e)

Library of Congress Control Number: 2014911126

CONTENTS

These memoirs are dedicated to the one who gives them all their meaning - Betty L. (Betts) MacDonald Harney, with whom these life experiences are shared, and with whom they became possible.

Acknowledgements

Listing those many who shared these stories as they were lived proves to be more than space and memory - as vivid as they may be - can accommodate. But I cannot neglect these earliest contributors to whatever success the author later achieved. The teachers who introduced me to the wonders of learning and using foreign language: Miss Perriens (beginning Latin) and Miss Haines (advanced Latin), Mr. Fred C. Mitchell, Lynn Classical High School Principal, and Mr. Bill Joyce, LCHS Head Athletic Coach and mentor to Classical's trophy winners, who gave us a taste for victory then and during other challenges which came along.

FOREWORD

OFFICE OF THE CHIEF OF STAFF
UNITED STATES AIR FORCE
WASHINGTON

29 March 1980

Mr. John R. Harney
8603 Powhatan Street
New Carrollton, Maryland   20784

Dear Jack

From cavalry to NSA policy direction --
your career has been broad and productive.   We
all owe you a great debt for your contributions
to the security of the country.   I wish there
were more men of your caliber -- we need them.
Best of luck to you and Betty.

Sincerely

LEW ALLEN, JR., General, USAF
Chief of Staff

THE EARLY YEARS

I was born the last of four children to William Henry Harney and Mary Agnes (Sullivan) Harney. Dorothy, the oldest child, was 12 years old when I was born, Bill (William, Jr.) was 10, and Marguerite was six.

Both mother and father had been born and raised in Lynn, Massachusetts, where I was also born. My mother's family (Sullivans and Foxes) had emigrated from County Cork, Ireland and my father's parents had emigrated from the Galway area—all of them had left Ireland in the bad years in the latter half of the 1800s.

Mother was the oldest of four children born to her parents; when they both died young, before she was 10, she took over much of the care for her brothers and sister in their foster home with the Fox family.

As was not uncommon in those days, she ended her schooling with grammar school, and began working in a shoe factory at about age 12. As she told us later, she didn't see the sun for much of her working days, going to work before sunup and leaving after sundown.

Father was the youngest of 13. His father was brother to the principal, and wealthiest, shoe manufacturer in Lynn, the country's major shoe center of that time. There were well-to-do Harneys throughout the North Shore area.

Other Harneys settled in this country; the most famous became a general in the Union Army, was involved (without distinction, I believe) in the Missouri compromise, became an Indian fighter, and—according to legend—met his end while chasing an Indian fugitive across some ice which could support an Indian but not a general. For his feats he left behind a mountain in the Dakota Black Hills and a lake in central Florida which bear his name.

Closer to home, two brothers (Martin and James) became Jesuit priests: James spent his life in the missions doing good works and Martin became a history professor at Boston College: as far as I know, neither had any mountains named after them—at least on this earth. Msgr. Martin did have a bit of family fame by returning to the old country on sabbatical to write the Harney history, hoping to find a famous king or two in the lineage—he returned early, discouraged and unfulfilled, when it is said his research through several generations could find "nothing but horse thieves and drunkards".

But the branch headed by my grandfather managed to escape any touch of wealth. Rumors were that Grandpa (Michael/Peter?) Harney was the disinherited black sheep of the clan, but no cogent explanation ever made it to me through the protective fence of the Irish family. All my grandparents predeceased my birth day.

Whatever the reason was, my father received no patrimony, and he, too, had to leave school at the end of the eighth grade to go to work in the shoe factory. Despite a good dose of native intelligence, he was unable to overcome this unfortunate start, and he spent his hard-working life grubbing out a subsistence living for his wife and us children.

Not that he did not try. He made several starts, and at one time was on his way to a respectable level of employment with the General Electric company in Lynn (the major employer in the area). I deduce that some unhappy involvement with the union played a part in keeping this from happening.

There were also rumbles of gambling and drinking in his youth (before I was born), most of which I was inadvertently briefed on during one or another of the pandemic fights which my parents were susceptible to during my time with them. Whatever the truth was, it couldn't have been as bad as it seemed, or as I believed it at the time . . .

Whether it was out of frustration or desperation, my father did engage in periodic drinking bouts—off-campus—during much of his later years. He did not, however, directly abuse any of us in any way.

By the time I was aware of things, his personal battle was almost lost. The Depression (among my earliest memories) sealed off any reasonable likelihood that my father could get on track again. He was able to get us through the Depression by working as a timekeeper with the WPA; later he went on working at various jobs, doing his part to keep the family together, ultimately in a job with a local retailer that gave him some satisfaction.

He did take pleasure in what his children were able to accomplish, and his grandchildren, to the extent he lived to see it. All of us—I in particular—wish he could've seen the days of our successes. But he died with only the suspicion that we might make it. I hope that his belief in Heaven has been realized, and that he has seen it after all.

At any rate, this basically nice man lived out his days without ever reaching his own potential. I did not realize how his life must've frustrated him, until he was in his last years. I sometimes weep for him now, now that it is too late . . . William Henry Harney, Sr. died in the hospital in Lynn at age 68, from heart failure. I flew in an airplane for the first time to be at his funeral.

Back to me. I grew up as a mother's boy. I had great affection for my mother, and she for me. She lavished on me the care and love due to "the baby", and which she for good reason, by her lights, no longer felt was owed to her husband.

I was in effect an only child—doubtless unexpected, but looked at as a joy for advancing years. My older sister Dot became a deputy mother and made sure I grew into the Apple of everyone's eye; this must have made my other sister Peg, only six years older, a bit uneasy, but she did not show it to me.

Brother Bill, 10 years older, was not a part of this until much later. In my early years he was out becoming a teenager and a young adult. He was not around often enough, nor did we have a structured enough family, for him to become a role model or much of a guiding force. So I remained a mother's (and older sister's) boy.

My mother was the strongest influence on my youth. The visible struggles she had with life, and her determination to make a home for us, made me want to do things to help, but much more, to avoid doing things to harm. The desire to please her—to get good grades and to be "a good boy"—shaped my character as much as anything else, both for good and not so good.

She was a strong woman. Celtic qualities abounded. Her whole life was her family. There were no friends, close or otherwise, that I could see. She had been brought up by strict Catholics, and although she was by my time no longer a churchgoer, the beliefs of her own youth governed her thoughts. The premature end of her schooling prevented her from taking advantage of a native intelligence, and the lack of any external influences kept my mother prisoner to the most prejudiced world of her immigrant Irish forebears.

She was, despite all that, a positive influence on me. Her unquestioned love, given without conditions, showed itself in many ways. She supported me in all things, ultimately even in those which she feared would harm me (like football). She went without the simplest things for herself in order to afford them for me. I owe her more than I can say, and, unfortunately, more than I ever made clear to her.

Mary Agnes Sullivan Harney died in the hospital after an operation which turned out to be for cancer. She was 84. Our last conversation was by phone from Munich with her in the hospital bed. I did manage to be with her at her funeral.

Next to mother, the most influence on me was exerted by sister Dorothy. Dot was really a "little mother". She helped me all through the years I spent at home, and was my greatest rooter. I believe she was the one who taught me to read before I entered the first grade.

Among many, many other things, I remember the suit she bought me so that I could graduate in style from Harvard. (This was obviously before the blue jeans-and-gown years which were to follow). Dot died in her bed, of an apparent heart attack in her 50th year—a very great loss to all of us. One of my life's regrets is that I was not able to arrange to return from Germany for her funeral. I mourned for her alone, in the quiet of St. Sebastian's Chapel in Frankfurt/Main.

Marguerite (sister Peg) and I grew up mostly apart. The six year difference was an enormous gap. I remember mostly her taking me to church with her on Sundays, and her concern that I not disgrace myself for her. But as we will see in later pages Peg and I grew up much closer as my own increasing age narrowed the gap.

In her last years, Peg was invalided by a combination of a heart problem (perhaps brought on by a severe childhood flu) and a regimen of prescribed drugs. She died at age 66 while I was on a business trip to Germany—I did return in time for her funeral.

Brother Bill was not a great factor in my growing up. The 10 year age difference made any meaningful communication unlikely. I did follow him around when I could, and some of his younger friends became older ones for me. It was not until well after the war that Bill and I really became brothers—and then only infrequently because Betty and I soon moved away.

As I reached the age of 10, sister Dot began her own family—a son Arthur and a daughter Janice. My mother and I spent much time helping out babysitting; there was less than two years between the grandchildren, and only 10 between Artie and me.

I became quite close to the young Arthur—kind of like his mother was to me, but never as much. He grew up to be a successful father and businessman after a solid Harvard education. Janice and I were not as close; her years have been much less successful than her brother's, but she is despite that a very nice, although troubled, person.

My mother never really accepted Dot's husband Arthur McCarthy. There were, it turned out, valid reasons for this, but in the best of cases Arthur would have had to be quite a guy to break through the barrier of not having been born into our family.

As bad as he appeared in my mother's eyes, Arthur was a Catholic. His co-in-laws, Peg's husband Mac (Irvin McKay), and Bill's wife Laura (Hodgdon) were not, and as penance they had to battle to gain acceptance from mother Harney. Both of them succeeded, as well they should have.

Betty, my own dear wife, came the closest to getting instant acceptance, and would have, I believe, if she had not sinned by stealing me, the baby of the family, away. But Betty benefited not only from her own winning ways, but also from the distance we put between ourselves and homebase when we moved to Washington. That and from her choice of parents, who my mother really liked.

CHORES AND EARLY WORK EXPERIENCE

They were not called chores in my family, but each of us had things to do to help out around the house. Among my earliest memories are the visits I made from our upstairs "tenement" (in my aunt Annie's house, where the family lived) to the dark cellar to fill a coal scuttle and scuttle with it back up the stairs.

The monsters I met on the way stayed with me for many years, but the kitchen coal stove which I fed was the only source of heat for our whole apartment. (Later on we did acquire a kerosene heater, which provided a certain amount of movable, very pungent warmth).

My second job was to empty the icebox pan, so that it did not overflow into our back hallway. The icebox was a pre-refrigerator arrangement, a cooler with 15 cents worth of ice a day, all of which filled the pan regularly. I was pleased and proud to be able to purchase from my pay in later years the family's first refrigerator.

In addition I helped my mother with sweeping and washing the floors, and watched as she did little household repairs. Whatever small skills I bring to the toolbox come from those hours when I watched her resolute, left-handed attack with a screwdriver or some other strange instrument which filled a drawer in our pantry.

Perhaps the least enjoyable of these tasks was having to go to the city outlet for surplus government food supplies. The family's low income qualified us for two cent milk, powdered, and various other foodstuffs at subsidized prices. Walking the mile or so home, carrying the telltale bags past some of my high school friends' houses was something of a trauma.

The first paying job I had was as a caddie at a local country club. I used to hitch rides to and from the club, and on good days would carry for 18 or 36 holes. 75 cents for one bag, $1.50 for double. Plus a 25 cent tip and-maybe a five cent cold drink at the turn!

I learned many things in those 12 year old days, some about golf on the course, some about the tipping habits of doctors and lawyers, but most of them in the caddie shack, about other, more titillating things. It was a valuable experience; however, I'm afraid the few paltry dollars I earned have cost me much in time and money I have returned to the game over the years.

At about the same time I was hired as a kitchen counselor (permanent KP!) at the Boy Scout summer camp in Amesbury—Camp Powell, I do believe. There was no money involved, but in return for long hours with pots and pans I received free board and room, plus access to camp facilities in the off hours. That was worth eight dollars a week in 1937 dollars. Just think if I had asked for GE stock instead!

Next was a job with a local milkman, to whom I provided unskilled help in loading his truck and making deliveries to local retail stores and restaurants. Apart from learning how to react when being picked up at 4 AM each day, this did not yield much valuable business experience.

But he paid me fairly, and he did arouse my interest by his repeated lament about missed opportunities with the girls: "if I only knew in high school what I know now". He did not impart to me what it was he now knew, so it was of no real benefit to the rest of my junior and senior high school days. Not that it, or much else for that matter, would've overcome the shyness of those years!

In high school I won a job as the school reporter for the local daily newspaper, the <u>Lynn Telegram</u>. Since most of my interests centered on sports activities, it was a natural for me.

As much as editor J. F. Williams (real name: Joe Finkel) might have wished it, I did not violate the secrets of the locker room—even though our coach was concerned enough, before I took the job for the second year, to remind me that I had "larger interests" at stake.

(As a matter of fact, the only time they were violated was by a planted story which had me replacing the key player on our team for the championship game—on a day when I was sick in bed and missed practice!)

The job was very interesting. I had to learn to type—a very high level of hunt and peck if I do say so, which I use even as we speak. It returned a reasonable stipend, computed at the rate of five cents per column inch. I wrote a lot of column inches! This early incentive to use three words where one would do has unfortunately stuck with me through the years.

But the job helped me to learn how to use my time. A full day of school, an afternoon of practice, some homework study, the walk downtown, composing and typing the copy, getting it in by the 11:00 PM (?) deadline, and the long walk home all made for a complete day.

As for the "larger interests" referred to by our coach—Bill Joyce, a really fine man and dean of area coaches—I did not risk very much. He meant the Lydia Pinkham scholarship of $1000 to the city's leading high school scholar athlete. Although I was in line for it, I suppose, as it turned out Lydia ran out of disposable funds in my senior year anyway.

The last job of my youth was with General Electric, the principal employer of the Lynn area. In the summer of 1942, after graduation from Lynn Classical and before entering Harvard in the fall, I worked mid-and swing shifts in the small electric motor department of the River Works plant.

My job was as a notch-press operator. It involved taking pre-stamped out metal discs (provided by the punch presses), and notching them on machines into various patterns as determined by dies provided and installed by (much!) more skilled workers. The process was noisy, hot, dirty, a bit dangerous, and brutally dull.

Each operation took a matter of a couple of seconds, and repeated itself through the lo-o-o-ng nights almost endlessly. The only challenges were to beat one's quota and to retain as many fingers as possible. Since we were paid on a piecework basis, these two challenges were not non-competing.

I learned that one could make a fair amount of money by steady application, but more importantly I got the idea that there had to be better ways to make money. There were lots of guys in white jackets walking around, moving in and out of important looking places, always occupied but clearly not on piecework; that's where I decided I wanted to be.

I also learned much else on that job—about people, about what "the sweat of one's brow" can mean, about the differences between skilled and unskilled labor, about some of the differences between management and all labor—but most of all, about how fortunate I was to have a shot at different worlds through education.

This particular job was important for a number of other reasons, not the least that it allowed me for a time to be the principal breadwinner in the family (Bill was in the Army, Dot had married, Peg was not on piecework, and our father was between jobs). Nonetheless, I left General Electric in the fall eager to enter Harvard.

I did not work for money during my freshman year, but just about at its end I took a temporary position with the U.S. Army. Although there was travel involved, the pay was not commensurate with the job description, the work was very arduous and employee safety standards left a lot to be desired. I'll cover it in more detail elsewhere.

After the war and my return to college, I did not have an outside job during my undergraduate semesters. The G.I. Bill took care of my modest wants at that time. But in between semesters I worked as a laborer (unskilled hardly describes my level of qualifications!) for my brother-in-law, Arthur McCarthy.

Arthur ran a small contracting business, mostly in asphalt paving of private home driveways and an occasional business parking lot. I learned how to work a grub hoe and to spread and rake stone dust and even to drive a power roller in the preparatory stages before applying the asphalt. Arthur seldom used me in the final raking and rolling of the asphalt—the raw materials were too expensive to put at risk!

But it was tough, hot, dirty, hard work. I got to like it, even though it was not to be my bag. There is an honesty to manual labor that I learned to respect. Most of all, there was nothing like the feeling of cleaning up at the end of the day and heading out to play ball in the cool of the evening, or just to goof off, knowing well that you had earned it.

In graduate school at BU, I earned walking around money by teaching German to undergraduates (I had a paying fellowship as a lecturer in German), and by tutoring PhD candidates through their language qualifying exams.

Tutoring at five dollars an hour, especially when I could get a class together, was not bad pay for a single guy; but I got married. That's covered elsewhere, but it led to my final part-time job and ultimately to my career in government.

I answered an ad for a sales job with a landscaping company. Actually it was a company that sold flowering plants, but used "free" landscaping services as a gimmick. After a one-day sales training course, I was qualified to sell landscaping plans to unsuspecting young marrieds who had bought into their first mortgage.

On my first day with the company I actually did sell one—really, I sold a couple of hundred dollars worth of plants whose names I scarcely recognized, from a catalog I had just paged through, to a couple who thought I was Johnny Appleseed himself!

I refused my commission, handed in my catalog, and decided to look elsewhere. The only value to this work experience was a lifelong distrust of "experts" who want to sell me <u>anything.</u>

But then I went on to my life's work—to be covered elsewhere.

SPORTS, SCHOOLING, AND EXTRACURRICULARS

These segments of my life have been closely intertwined. The mix is in fact responsible for many of the good things I have been fortunate enough to enjoy.

In grammar school and well into junior high, sports activities were informal; i.e., they were not institutionalized into peewee leagues, little boys and girls clubs games, or the like.

Not that they were unshaped—it's just that we kids did our own shaping: organizing, team formation, site selection, scheduling, equipment providing, etc. etc. Much of it was the team from our street (our street was Moulton Street) against their streets, but we played variations on that theme, too.

There was track and field, football, baseball, volleyball, wrestling (lots of wrestling!), boxing, ice hockey, and plenty of running and jumping. We did not play basketball on our own—and there was no tennis on our street! Swimming was something we did if we got knocked over by a wave or fell out of a boat, but certainly not on purpose!

Equipment was dredged up from somewhere, usually from older brothers, and taped baseballs and repaired bats and ragged gloves were the norm. Even our ice skates were mostly hand-me-downs. (I recall that as late as when I was trying out for the Harvard varsity baseball team, the glove I used was borrowed from a friend's brother).

The closest our neighborhood teams came to uniforms was a pair of used football pants (with real pads) which my mother bought me for 75 cents at the Morgan Memorial store, and a cardboard-like helmet which one of the other boys had acquired from somewhere. We were the only "uniform" players I can remember, although there may have been one or two others with cleats.

But we played real games with real rules, serving mostly as our own referees and officials, and we learned how to play the games, and how to win and how to lose. And when we did win or lose we were responsible only to ourselves. It was a lot easier then . . .

I began school at age 6, in the first grade of Tracy Elementary in Mrs. Vaughn's class. Old enough to be my grandmother, she gave us all a great start.

It was a public school (Dot and Bill had gone to Catholic Parochial school through their early grades), and it concentrated on reading, writing, and arithmetic. Somehow I had learned to read before entering first grade—there were no kindergartens for us—so it was mostly a matter of arithmetic and writing.

Early school years were mostly uneventful, except for a broken wrist (sledding) in first grade, where my injury made me a celebrity and caused me to write left-handed for a critical while. My penmanship has never recovered! Nor has my taste for celebrity.

I remember most of the teachers: Mrs. Vaughn, Mrs. McCarthy, Ms. Fowler, Miss Sorokin, Miss Turner. They all did their jobs well—although I recall that Miss Sorokin had a tough time getting me to understand long division (my only "D").

The skills we learned in those first six years sufficed to carry us through the rest of our schooling. The extra-curricular major event was that I (just barely) earned my way onto the school traffic patrol team in sixth grade.

My only other firm memory has to do with my extreme bashfulness: I used to blush at the slightest attention directed at me. Early on, to help combat this, the teachers used to have me read aloud at every opportunity.

Along about fourth grade I remember reading to some younger children on a night we were putting on a school play. The book was Barrie's <u>Peter Pan</u>, and when I came to the phrase "silly ass", the trauma of saying those words aloud set the teacher's efforts back about six more years!

As for the rest of elementary school, it was a breeze, except for a serious battle with long division. But that, too, passed. They were happy days. Although we were poor—we would now be well below the poverty line—we were all poor together, and we consequently did not sense deprivation. We were able to accept our lot and enjoy the good things we had—friends, play, the occasional toy, and the innocence of the very young.

And there was no rancor at the many things we did not have, perhaps because we were not constantly made aware that we did not have them. That does not mean by any means that we didn't plan to do great things when we grew up, but the pressures of doing them "right now" had not yet developed. There is much to be said for the blessings of the pre-television world.

After-school memories had to do with playing ball in the streets—upsetting some of the residents to the point where they would call the cops to break up our games. One of the policemen, a beefy Irishman named Kennedy, took that important responsibility so seriously that he once chased me into my own house, up the stairs, and only stopped when I had achieved the sanctuary of my mother's skirts.

Ofc. Kennedy never did that again—on the other hand, that was the last confrontation of any significance I ever had with the police. It clearly did us both some good.

Not that we didn't come close. All of the boys in the neighborhood had to sample forbidden fruits growing on the pear and apple trees behind all those challenging picket fences. So sample we did, and many the close call and ripped out pant legs we got in return!

It must have been during these years that my mother became convinced I would never live to see high school. She later told me that she never saw me when I was not running, usually in dangerous places, so she had to force herself to stop looking. A likely story!

Before Junior High began, the family moved out of Aunt Annie's house into a tenement on Boston Street. It made for a longer walk to school, but it was a much nicer place to live—all things being relative, of course. Our new digs did offer a much more modern—for the time—bathroom, which had a real bath tub. The years of Saturday night baths in an oversized basin, located for the event rather publicly in the center of the kitchen floor, were over, but never to be forgotten!

In the three years of Junior High School the world begat some other serious changes: moving from classroom to classroom, the homeroom adventure, puberty and all its miseries and joys, advancing sports competition to new levels (mostly still without adult supervision). Seventh-to-ninth grade was for us the beginning of really growing up.

In the classroom: algebra, mechanical drawing, shop work, chorus. I did not do too well in shop; I was among the last to make the doorbell ring in our electricity exercise. (I have often recalled that ruefully in later years—especially when called to "manage" W-J's brilliant engineering talents as we tried to move out smartly against the electromagnetic world market).

I was better in algebra and Latin, especially in Latin. Miss Perriens was the teacher who opened the mysteries of foreign languages to me. Her beginning Latin courses are really the foundation of whatever professional successes I have achieved. Her encouragement made advancement possible, and her threats made it imperative!

Two thespian adventures—singing a solo as the "older man" in our class operetta, and playing in a number of radio dramas (broadcast live on

Boston's WAAB radio station!)—fertilized the egg of public speaking, whose fruit was to help nourish me in later career years.

Finally the first organized sports activity—a citywide junior high track meet—brought me the first tangible return from a sports competition. It was an ice cream bar, bought by the coach for winning the 220 yard dash . . . an award which created a lifelong taste for victory in sports and elsewhere.

Next it was on to Lynn Classical High School, and to the three defining years of my education and future life.

On the day I entered Classical I signed up to try out for football. High school football was really big in New England, where few graduates went on to college and local identification was still with the high school teams.

All 129 pounds (and 5'10") of me made the team. At first, only on the scrubs which served as daily fodder for the varsity players, but when first-term grades came out, Coach Joyce moved me out of my chosen pass-catching-and-being-thumped end position into a kind of quarterback-in-waiting role.

He had been impressed at my 4.0 grade average (despite the daily thumping he witnessed), and, convinced that brains made good quarterbacks, began to make the transformation. Boley Dancewicz, our sophomore quarterback and a solid average student (who went on to quarterback and captain Notre Dame), caused both the coach and me to revise our plans!

How fortunate—at least partly as a result of not starting me at quarterback, our 1939-40-41 football teams won two State and one New England championship. But I did get in enough time to letter as a halfback. And as a second-team regular, I played for the only team which (in practice) once beat our otherwise unconquered varsity.

In the meantime, school went on for three years. I joined all the activities that would have me—became president of the Pan-American Club, sports editor of the school quarterly, member of the debating team, officer of the Honor Society, school drama club actor, Junior - and Senior-Class President, and in the end Class of 1942 valedictorian.

But sports were still my favorite fruit! I was able to letter in both football and baseball (varsity first baseman and second-team quarterback/half back), run some track, and act as sports reporter/groupie for basketball and the rest.

Grade-point levels remained at 4.0 for most of the three years, but fell a bit in the spring of senior year when solid geometry and a heavy traveling baseball schedule bumped heads. Faculty help got us through, although I still would not want to risk my life on the math that I was credited with learning that final quarter!

Lynn Classical had a solid faculty and staff, headed by an outstanding person, educator and mentor, Principal Fred Mitchell. He was fire and ice, old New England integrity and Yankee solidity. His students respected him before all others. And after more than a quarter-century as Classical's principal, he retired to genteel poverty in Maine . . .

He supported my desire to go on to college, encouraged me when I needed encouragement, goaded me when I needed goading, and was the first to learn and to rejoice in the good news that I had received a four-year national scholarship to Harvard.

And well he might have rejoiced: of the 36 Harvard national scholarships awarded nationwide in 1942, two went to Lynn Classical students. David I. (for Izzie) Balakar—runner-up for valedictorian—received the other. Izzie went on to win a PhD in physics from Harvard, founded his own electronics firm, and amassed millions of dollars.

A word about Izzie. We both graduated from Harvard in the class of 1946, although I was delayed by World War II for several years. In 1960, I think, we read about I. David Balakar in a Time magazine article about America's youngest millionaires. David (no longer Izzie) was credited with a gross worth of some $36 million. It has become a family joke to wonder how much greater success he would've achieved if only he, instead of I, had been valedictorian.

On a more serious note, I think a word is in order about some advantages of growing up and being schooled in the years before World War II. We did not know it, but we were multicultural before the word had been invented.

In the New England I knew, there were no serious racial tensions. There were no really serious ethnic tensions. This was true despite the existence of deep economic class divisions. In my opinion it was not until the postwar growth of the middle class, in which many members of some ethnic and most minority racial groups were left behind, that yesterday's racial tensions in the South permeated to many other areas of the nation.

Large numbers of today's middle classes—me among them—were in my youth part of the great underclasses. We were all of us together—Irish, Italian, Negroes, Lithuanians, Chinese, French, Latinos, Jews, Scots—poor working stiffs. We didn't know any better, and we were in the same boat economically. The piece of the pie that we had any chance at was just not worth fighting each other about.

But after the war, when the gates of opportunity were opened by great industrial and education explosions, the part of the pie which we all had a look at had grown considerably. Competition for a home and a car or two and a pleasant life became real possibilities for many who just half a generation before would have had no chance at all.

But many were left behind. Some had become so mired in the mud of the 30s that they had lost hope, and with it ambition. Others had by necessity or choice chosen other courses. But whatever the reasons, major divisions opened and grew larger in our society. It led to the breakdowns of the 50s, the great attempts to remedy in the 60s, and the remissions and tragic failures over the last decades extending into our present days.

I apologize for this wandering afield. The point I wanted to make was that these high school years were privileged to be simpler and much more wholesome than they can ever be again. How fortunate we were in our unrecognized misfortune . . .

With graduation from high school, a whole segment of my life came to a successful end. I recall worrying, true to my Irish heritage even in the midst of all the bright promise of those days, if things could hardly get any better, they could certainly get worse. And in the background—not yet heard in any reality—boomed the guns of a world war yet to be fought . . .

But on to that, and to the University days, elsewhere.

First row, left to right: Pete Spyropoulos, Bob Mikzenas, Bob McNulty, Gasper Urban, Ben Glowik, Boley Dancewicz, and Tom Costley. Second row   Faculty manager George Skillin, 'ine coach Harold Zimman, Ernie Savory, Al Saulenas, Mecca Smiarowski, Tom Brown, Coach William Joyce and Principal Fred Mitchell. Third row: Walter McCabe, Norman Dodge, Jack Harney, Bill Murphy, Ray McNulty, Joe Russell, Tony Gallo, Joe Kasle, and Jo~ McGinn. Fourth row: Mitchell Dembrowski, Stanley Stopper, Fran Kelley, Ted Weilgus, John Zales, Bob Zimman, Bill Magee, Bill Murray, Albert Reppucci.

LYNN CLASSICAL FOOTBALL AND THE ORANGE BOWL TRIP

A recent talk with son John reminded me of an early visit to Florida, when the Lynn Classical High School 1941 football team was awarded a trip to the Orange Bowl game of 1941-1942. I thought a brief account of that trip would sort of cap off the discussion of sports and schooling in the previous chapter.

The Lynn Classical Football teams of 1940 and 1941 were among the best the school had ever put together. In 1940 Classical won the State Championship, and in 1941 we won both the state and the New England championships. As one result, the school gave the lettermen of 1941 an all-expenses-paid trip to Miami where we would see the Orange Bowl game of that season. This trip was paid for out of the income from our home games. The WPA had in the late 1930s built the first-class 20,000-seat Manning Bowl in Lynn, which our successful teams filled to overflowing for each game. Income from ticket sales paid for our practice and game uniforms, shoes, pads, and a brand-new set of underwear and socks for every game. It also was enough to cover our trip expenses, including a $5.00 per diem stipend for the days we spent in Florida. A princely sum for those times.

The trip itinerary included a scheduled overnight boat trip to New York City (unhappily replaced by train travel when Pearl Harbor intervened and pleasure boats were canceled); and overnight stay in New York; travel by bus to Washington, DC and another overnight stay; a train trip to Jacksonville, Florida (including Pullman berths, which we thoughtlessly—but unintentionally—trashed when the pillows shed their feathers during a childish pillow fight en route); and a final leg by bus to Miami with stops in St. Augustine and Palm Beach. Viewing the Orange Bowl Parade and attending the game between Georgia Tech and Texas Christian University (won handily by Frank Sinkwich and his Georgia Tech teammates) were as exciting as expected. An unexpected benefit for us was that our Lynn Classical football sweaters were white with a big red "C"—close enough to the TCU sweaters to attract more than our share of coeds who attended!

It was a fantastic trip, one of a lifetime for some of our teammates and one of indelible memories for all of us. And given the ravages of the war which was to follow for most of us, it was the last highlight for at least one life . . . One of the low lights—which most of us were unaware of until much later—was the ugly environment south of Washington DC which prevented our two black teammates from accompanying us into the racist deep South. The team spirit of Tom Brown and Ernie Savory, two of our most valuable starting players, in fact enabled the rest of us to go on. Faced with the choice posed by our great principal, Mr. Fred Mitchell, of whether he should cancel the trip for all, or make "acceptable" alternative arrangements for them to spend their prize time in DC, they chose the latter, had a good time, and never raised the issue publicly. Mr. Mitchell, with the endorsement of Tom and Ernie, decided to let the rest of us proceed. I have no doubt that our team would have voted to go elsewhere had the choice been offered, but these two black teammates—with one of whom I without compunction shared locker space—made that unnecessary.

A final sidebar: we were accompanied/chaperoned by coach Bill Joyce and assistant coach Hal Zimman, along with faculty manager Ralph Skillins and history teacher Judokus Van den Noort. Mr. Van den Noort was commissioned by the Lynn Item (the smaller of our two daily newspapers) to write a daily account of the trip, which he was to mail in at the close of each day. The other paper, the Lynn Telegram-News, commissioned me to do the same, but authorized me to file my daily story by Western Union telegraph. I had a built-in scoop each day of the trip, which Mr. Van den Noort accepted like the gentleman he was. I still have some copies of the front-page by-lined stories the Telegram printed. On rereading them, I can see why they were never considered for Pulitzer awards—but then, neither were Mr. Van den Noort's. I don't know what he was paid, but my five cents per column inch—amplified by copious high-school-level adjectives—brought some felicitous pocket money.

COLLEGE AND UNIVERSITY

From early days it seems, I had wanted to "go to college". Perhaps I recognized it was something the family hoped I would do, although there was no way to get to it without serious (probably total) outside help. I do remember that there was not a time that the whole family was not fully supportive of the idea. After all, I was the last "white hope" of this branch of the Harney's.

Dorothy was as bright as she could be—as was Peg—but neither of them had the slightest chance to go on to college. Although both did well in high school, the combination of working class prejudice against higher schooling for women, the need for them to work to help support the family, and the traditional wife and mother roles completely excluded college from their game plans.

Brother Bill was also very bright, but had been bothered from childhood with an embarrassing eczema condition which seem to have had the effect of keeping him from any track which would have exposed him to public attention. He did win scholarship help to attend a local business college (Burdette), but his condition worsened and he was forced to drop out.

All of them, Dot, Bill, and Peg went on to prove themselves in various jobs, advancing as well as they could through brute force, hard work and intelligence. But the Depression and the family's inability to help them help themselves kept them all from realizing their potentials.

That left me. I accepted the fact that I would have to be the one. The family accepted the fact that I would have to be the one. And although I never remember talking about how and where all this was to happen, it apparently went without saying that I was the college graduate-designate.

Through a mix of sports and extracurricular activities and excellent grades (I am reporting, not bragging!), I became in high school a prime candidate for scholarship assistance. To all of us in Lynn in those days, that meant competing for the Lydia Pinkham Award, the top scholarship prize we knew about.

Lydia Pinkham (who manufactured a slightly alcoholic tonic for "women's problems" in her Lynn factory) had established a $1000 award, rotating between the two public high schools in Lynn. 1942 was to be Classical's year, and I set my cap for that goal.

The only thing was, early in the year it was announced that the Pinkham Award was no longer to be offered. The Depression had struck again! Plan B had to be developed.

I had for some time hoped to go to Harvard. This desire was stoked when I won the local Harvard Club Red Book award in junior year. I had applied for acceptance, and in the process I also applied for scholarship help as a matter of course, without believing I had a chance at it.

After all, Lydia would get me through the first year or so, and we'd manage somehow.

Acceptance to Harvard required certain minimum SAT scores (even then they were around!). So I boned up pretty vigorously before the exams—especially in the suspect math areas—and got some very high scores. So high that, in conjunction with the extracurricular activities, they produced a four year all-expenses-paid National Scholarship.

I recall that coach Joyce broke the news to me between innings of a baseball game. It was ironic that he should do so, since he had been the one to warn me about not risking the Pinkham Prize by taking the school reporter job! Principal Mitchell soon added his warm congratulations, and a very surprised, very overwhelmed young Irish lad made his way home that evening.

It was off to Cambridge at the end of summer, and the beginning of the rest of my life. The scholarship paid tuition (in those days an incredible, by current prices, $400 a year!), room rent, meals, and most fees. Since I was within commuting distance I was considered a day student, and the room was for study purposes only. Meal allowances were adjusted commensurately.

My first day brought me to Harvard Square, where I was to meet my three new (study) roommates. I met one, a genial fellow named Ray Brown, who approached me with the greeting "You must be Harney; I can tell by the map of Ireland on your face!" It got better and better with Ray as time went on.

The second, another Irishman—this one studious—named Larry Hyde proved to be a solid, serious classmate. (He later became a very successful businessman, ultimately in the automotive industry, fired in the crucible of the Harvard Business School).

The third, Robert Warshaw, never did put much of an imprint on me, which says more about me than it does of him. I lost track of him after the first semester, but I believe he went on to do well somewhere.

The first semester was a whirl. I had thought to become a Classics major—with Latin and Greek and an academic career. I did take a course in Latin, from a typical absent-minded professor named Pease, but I decided to take beginning German in place of beginning Greek. This minor decision shaped the rest of my life—and, perhaps as you may read in another segment—probably prolonged it by decades!

Whatever the reasons, I was able to achieve the Dean's List status required to ensure continuation of the scholarship into the second semester of freshman year. I kept that status through a foreshortened second semester, and went off to serve in World War II with the knowledge that—if I survived—I could return as a National Scholarship holder into that uncertain future.

The War did many bad things, but among its minor casualties was any semblance of the traditional college years we had hoped for. To begin with there was, even as we enrolled, the uncertainty as to how and when we were to be involved in the fighting.

There was the bloated size of the class of 1946—the largest in Harvard's history to that date, albeit destined to be drastically reduced by war's mindless cropping. The numbers caused an unHarvard-like crowding and an unseemly haste in the gentlemanly pace one had been led to expect.

As the second semester unfolded, decisions to be made about whether to enlist straight off, to sign up for various officer training programs, to wait out the draft, etc. etc. And as we watched the war unfold in the bad days of 1942 and early 1943, these last months at school were both uncomfortable—in the knowledge that we were not doing our duty to country and flag—and foreboding in that we knew we were living the last days of a time that was not going to return.

We lived the artificially halcyon days of the Harvard that was: meals served in the House Dining rooms on linen, eaten on silver service, coffee in the common rooms with the Master, serious (if presumptuous) discussions with the Senior Fellow, ready access to much of the world's knowledge, and the time to be concerned with identity development and philosophies and cabbages and Kings!

We found time for sports and other recreation (Fenway Park and Durgin Park, the blandishments of Radcliffe and Wellesley and the fleshpots of Scollay Square—although we were much too ingenuous and far too broke to be very blandished); there was even time for the occasional round of golf, and the posh squash court competition.

Squash rackets was, along with the decision to study German, the defining happening of my freshman year—and certainly of my life. I met a new friend and classmate through my ignorance of what those anemic looking tennis rackets were for. When I asked him, he told me, and we ended that day by playing my first game of squash, the first event of a friendship which lasted a lifetime.

He was, of course, Chuck (Chick—Charles P.) MacDonald, roommate, close friend, and ultimately brother-in-law. I must say it up front: it is a rare family which can produce a Chuck and a Betty out of the same gene pool! I was fortunate to be Chuck's friend, and I have been outrageously lucky to spend my married years with Betty. But more about Betty after the war. After all, when I was a freshman at Harvard, she was still in high school, and under close wraps!

Many of the details of freshman year are clouded. I recall isolated events, but no coherent screenplay can be evoked. My German A instructor was an exchange faculty member from the University of Leeds (England); he must've been pretty good because my German A German has stuck with me all these years.

My English A instructor was a true liberal arts man—a published poet in fact, Delmar Schwartz. He was the first of many to tell me my prose style was wordy, but what I remember most about him is that he actually used the phrase "postprandial somnolence" in a casual sentence!

I recall two events from my ROTC training. The minor happening was when I accidentally fired a target pistol into the ceiling (a neat hole appeared in the heating duct) of the ROTC basement pistol range. I did not qualify for the medal . . .

The major event occurred when I stepped on the accelerator instead of the brake of a 2 1/2 ton truck, narrowly missing my instructor (Capt. Sherman Miles Jr, son of MajorGeneral Sherman Miles), ran through a ditch and knocked a hole in the fence surrounding the stables which housed our field artillery unit's horses. They were soon shipped out (some say it was my fault!), and I was not asked to drive the truck again.

In all fairness, I had never had any instruction in driving, and I had learned all I knew from watching others. And I had handled the truck up until then (in fact, I didn't miss the brake—I just had the truck in a forward gear instead of reverse when I gave it the gas!).

Not long after that my draft notice arrived. I had decided to wait it out after my mother put the kibosh on my desire to enlist in the Army

Air Corps—too dangerous, she said. While others got into officer training programs like the V12, etc., staying on at Harvard or some other college, at least for a while, Ray Brown and Phil Jefferson and I decided to just go in and fight. Ah, sweet, naïve youth!

One other happening: the college decided to accept our April Hour exam grades as final marks for the semester if we had to leave for the Services before finals. So once we passed the April Hours, it was off to the golf course for all of us!

One week before I was to report to the Army, I was struck in the shin by a five iron swung by a classmate; all I could think of as I crumpled to the ground was damn! I won't be able to get into the Army and I'll have to take the dreaded finals . . .

But my shin healed in time, and it was off to the War, with one year of Harvard under my belt! Back after a slight pause of three years—and most of a lifetime . . .

Pvt. John R. Harney - 1943

Author with Mother Mary, Sister Peg, and Father William Harney -1943

ARMY I — OFF TO THE WAR

With a tender shin and a light heart, I headed toward new experiences in the Army which had I but known, wouldn't have made either my shin or my heart feel better. I said goodbye to close Harvard friends and classmates in—where else, Harvard Square.

I remember only how Ray Brown and Phil Jefferson and I stood waiting for the last MTA subway train we would see for a long while, renewing our promise to each other not to interrupt our duty to our country by anything as unworthy as more schooling. Then Ray Brown performed his deliciously funny last clowning act as we stood on the platform, and off we went . . .

At the Selective Service Center in Boston, I went through the protocols of signing up, taking the oath, being examined physically (I learned I had pesplanus second degree, but also learned—to my irrational joy— that would not keep me out of the Army).

In fact, after some testing, I ran the gamut of the Services: each one had its own cubicle, where they could solicit new recruits from the day's catch. Marine Corps had first choice—I declined; Navy had second choice—I declined again; the Army had third choice—and I had run out of options.

After a week or so at home, it was off to Fort Devens. Parting with parents and family was painful, but all I can remember was my favorite uncle, Henry Sullivan, as he hugged me and pressed $20 into my hand as I boarded the train.

The trip from Lynn to Ayer couldn't have lasted much more than an hour, but it was long enough for me to lose the $20 in a card game. My lifelong distaste for gambling began in that hour, although I didn't effectively act on it until some months later.

At Devens we were issued (with, as the Brits would add) uniforms and passed through a series of tests, including the important ASAT series, the Army's IQ measurement. Other aptitude tests were administered, and I was surprised to learn of my flair for Morse code. So was the Army.

Although my ASAT scores were well above requirements for Officer Candidate School (OCS), the Army had created a surplus of second lieutenants. Casualty figures showed you can never have enough of them in combat, but the Army had temporarily closed its OCS lists anyway. That left radio school for me, to cash in on that Morse code aptitude.

Apparently, the radio school available was at Fort Riley, Kansas, home of the U.S. Army cavalry. It was also the home of the Cavalry Replacement Training Center. So it was off to Kansas in a crowded troop train, across middle America for the first time, through seriously flooded flatlands. But we made it. I recall looking out at sleeping village after sleeping town (the rail lines passed directly through them) and wondering for the first time at the spaciousness of this great country.

I was also struck for the first time (of many since) by the thought of how many stories and how many families were housed in the darkened homes, and wondering about them and their lives—all of which would be lived without any knowledge or concern about mine—and especially about what emergencies lay behind the occasional ominously lighted window. Travel through a darkened world still does me like that!

Finally, arrival at Fort Riley, accompanied by the chorus of "You'll be sor-r-y" from those who had arrived hours or days earlier.

The next 13 or so weeks introduced us to the Army. I recall them in a series of vignettes, faded a bit by time, but preserved enough to have made it through the decades.

There was the first KP duty (terrible) and the first G.I. barracks cleaning (not quite so bad) and the first shots (I caught a little bit of every disease except smallpox) and the first night march (almost fun). There was also the first special equipment issue: boots and extra-wide-bottom raincoats, to allow spreading out over saddles and horses' rears!

The first four weeks were spent in basic basic, learning to drill, march (day and night), shoot, crawl under barbed wire while under machine gun fire, use gas masks, run through obstacle courses, and especially how to suppress most thinking processes in favor of automatic response to orders.

Learning to shoot was great, since I had never done much of that (except for shooting a hole in Harvard's ROTC ceiling!). And I enjoyed the competitive aspects. We fired the M1 Garand rifle (although we had been issued the World War I Springfield 03—30 caliber), the 45 caliber automatic pistol, and the 30 caliber (modified for 22 caliber ammunition) machine gun, all on ranges for record.

I qualified in all three, as sharpshooter with the rifle, expert with the machine gun, and marksman with the pistol. This authorized me to wear three (!) medals, which I took much pride in doing.

I recall that as one part of the M1 qualification we fired at targets 500 yards away. No problem for me, since I'd been gifted with very good eyesight, but my shooting partner could not see the targets.

He was the old man of our group, a 27-year-old ex-playboy from New York City. We got him through the exercise by pointing out a lonesome pine tree—probably the only one in that part of Kansas—and telling him to fire at the white blur beneath it. I don't know what happened to him in later years, but I always hoped it didn't involve shooting a rifle in earnest.

After basic basic we split our days between radio school in the morning, and horse cavalry training in the afternoons (and whatever the First Sgt. thought up for the nights!)

I learned how to send and copy Morse code (at 25-27 wpm), the basics of radio net operation, and a little about ciphers, using the M-209—my only brush with cryptology until my NSA years. What I remember the most was the effort required to operate the manually-cranked generator; that was my first involvement with uninterrupted power supplies!

More fun, and more work, with the afternoons learning to be cavalry troopers. I really enjoyed riding, although the care and comfort of the horse was another matter. Rule number one said the cavalry was designed more for the horses than the riders, and rule number two said the cavalryman is distinguished from an infantryman only by his horse-which is the principal reason for rule number one!

Two events stick out in memory: one was the old Army drill which required you to drop your stirrups and ride out at a slow trot; my old (27 years, remember!) buddy used to come home in the evening and peel his bloody underwear away from his thighs. I was not bloody, but very sore!

The second was the battle with the enlisted men's saddle, the modified Stimson split rail model, designed to protect the horse's spine, and to toughen the inside of the rider's thighs. That's when I first noted the real difference between officers and enlisted men.

The officers—really an impressive group at Fort Riley, some of them with their own polo ponies for Sunday matches—rode on English saddles. We envied them so much that we used to ride a bus to nearby Manhattan, Kansas on our free weekends, and rent horses with English saddles. It was worth it!

Halfway through our cavalry training, we received new mounts from Montana. They were great horses—at least mine was (I called him/it Constipated, because he/it wasn't)—but they had not been exposed to small-arms fire.

My most vivid memory of Kansas came on the day we were to fire our pistols for record over a mounted course. As the acting squad leader of the first squad of the first Troop (Company, to non-horsemen), I volunteered to fire the first practice round.

I recall urging Constipated from a trot to a smooth canter, leading out over his/its withers, taking the target in sight and squeezing off the practice round directly into the middle of the silhouette target. Then all hell broke loose, as Constipated set out at a full gallop toward Western Kansas.

I jounced and bounced, trying to regain control with the one free hand, but finally gave up and ditched the pistol so that I could bring him/it under control. I returned to the rest of the troop, fully expecting the Sgt. to relieve me of my "command" on the spot for having tossed the pistol.

Instead, I heard him say, "that's what a true trooper has to do, to keep from accidentally shooting his mount!" Thus I learned early on not to pay too much attention to letters of commendation and the like . . .

We finished our mounted training with a couple of Friday afternoon parades (passing in Review at slow trot while the band played <u>Pop Goes The Weasel</u> doesn't fade from memory). I believe we all missed the end of that sort of pageantry.

I also recall buying my spurs and wearing them into Junction City (where I also had gotten deathly ill from a slug of bootleg white lightning) on the day after our night march—on foot—of 25 miles, extended to 27 because the lieutenant got lost. In a movie house that day I tripped on my spurs into the lap of a grizzled major, who gave me a great lesson: "Trooper, when you learn how to wear your spurs, you can put 'em on!"

Our radio training ended somewhat less spectacularly. We set up a radio net for a Battalion-level exercise. The net operated out of the armored recon cars (predecessors to half tracks). I was net control and radioman for the Battalion Commander over the two day maneuver.

The only problem was, we were told to operate in voice mode, while all of our training had been in Morse communications. A combination of that, some poor radio equipment, and a lot of static kept us from ever getting the net satisfactorily set up. The CO sent a lot of commands by motorcycle—as he had done in the good old War . . .

By that time, we had been put on orders for the First Cavalry Division, an honor in itself. But before we could join the division and move on out, together with horses, to Australia, a Higher Power intervened.

Fort Riley HQ announced some vacancies for the Army Specialized Training Program (ASTP) in language and engineering. I took and passed the German exam (bless German A!), passed the required ASAT scores for ASTP (10 points higher than for OCS), and was accepted.

A week later we were in a cattle truck on our way to the University of Nebraska in Lincoln—thus ending Army I.

ARMY II – AUGUST 43-FEBRUARY 44

I left the cavalry in an appropriate vehicle, I guess—an uncovered cattle truck. I don't remember the details, but a group of us were whisked, in what must've been just moderate discomfort, through the summer's heat from Fort Riley in Kansas to the campus of the University of Nebraska in Lincoln, Nebraska.

The trip may have been uncomfortable, but the objective was well worth it. We were deposited at the Love Library (not a description, alas, of the activity there), where we were assigned bunks in the stacks. I don't know where the books had gone, but the bunks were waiting for us.

The Army Specialized Training Program had been established to provide trained people in languages and engineering (and possibly other specialties as well) for use by the Army in various anticipated assignments overseas, probably in occupation tasks when and if the war had been won, or in war areas if it had not. I don't think it made much difference, because the program was terminated before any conclusions could be reached.

Small matter to us in the sunshine of the Lincoln campus! We had left the barking of noncoms giving us all manner of partially unintelligible, partially irrational commands, in favor of a university campus setting, where we had a chance to live as civilized human beings for a while.

We lived in both worlds for the five or so months we were allowed to be there. We were a sort of paramilitary presence in a scholastic environment—kind of a ghost at the party. We had access to the University milieu where we studied and wandered among the true students, and yet we were soldiers in all other ways, including standing reveille in -20° and going through other Army folderol of bed checks, uniforms, and other things I have long since forgotten.

Yet it was a great experience. I recall my first unofficial assignment was to represent a number of Ivy League colleagues in a telephone approach to a randomly selected sorority. It worked! The Harvard-Dartmouth-Princeton liaison with the University of Nebraska Tri-Delts was one of the grand successes of the ASTP experiment—of course, it was moderated by the times we lived in, and our liaisons were in no way worthy of the term in today's meaning. But they were great fun and made up in some measure for the college life we had left behind.

The combination of being together with other Ivy Leaguers and my pronounced distaste for alcohol at the time led to my learning to drink beer (a Nebraskan potent brew called "Stite") as fast as I could so that I could avoid the taste. This had the fortunate side effect that I quickly won the Ivy League chug a lug championship—the current title holder at that time was an ASTP student from Dartmouth—or was it Princeton?

The unfortunate side effects are better left to your own imagination. But we had many a pleasant Saturday evening at the old (then new) Cornhusker Hotel, where we played classic drinking games like Cardinal Puff and Crew Race until it was time to move to a nearby steakhouse, where we could have a monster T-bone with fixings and yet another Stite, for about $1.10 including tip.

Oh, yes, the classroom work. We did study much of the time. I recall learning some important things about the German area and language, though most of it was a reprise of our freshman (German A) course at Harvard. There was also a good deal about German history and culture.

It brings to mind a quiz on the German military, in which I identified "Keil and Kessel"—a German maneuver of thrust and encirclement—as two prominent Generals from the Afrika Korps. I was better as a linguist. We also published a class quarterly in German (I think we got one and two thirds issues out).

Not all of the students were born linguists, although the percentage was pretty high. One who was not was one of my closest buddies at UN, a Dartmouth hockey player from Medford. I helped him squeeze through the qualifying exams. But as in the case of the New Yorker who fudged his way through the rifle qualifying shoot, I hoped my Dartmouth friend would never have to use his German in anger!

But he did! Near the end of the war in Europe, as an infantryman with an advanced US unit, he was called upon to serve as interpreter when the US forces met the Russians at the Elbe. No English-speaking Russians nor Russian-speaking Americans could be found, so the forces made do with two German-speaking counterparts, one of whom, as noted was my Dartmouth friend. I have been bemused for some time by the thought that the Cold War was due in some part to the level of communication in that first meeting!

While we were still in Lincoln, my buddy and I set a record of sorts for the 100 yard dash carrying a buddy: 21 or 22 seconds as I recall, although since I was the carrier I may not be the most reliable source.

Just before the hammer fell, I got my first and only stateside leave—two weeks around Christmas which I used to go home to Lynn. Before I could go I made my only request for funds (since that first, ill-fated $20 from Uncle Henry). I recall it as $20, which I needed to have a pair of cavalryman's breeches tailored for me. It arrived, and I still have the breeches!

Of the long train ride home I recall only a lengthy evening stop in Albany, where I wrangled an invite to a nurses' dance at a local hospital. I don't think my dancing wowed them, but my new britches and my boots <u>and spurs</u> gave us plenty of dancing room!

The leave time at home was a sort of tearful family reunion, interrupted by some fried clam dinners and a wonderful evening with sister Peg at the Operetta in Boston, where we experienced <u>The Student Prince</u> for the first magical time.

Going back to Lincoln was highlighted by an afternoon in Chicago, in which on the way from one rail station to the other, I filled the time with (a) a horseback ride along the shore of Lake Michigan, (b) ten pin bowling at some enormous bowling theater, and (c) a pub crawl of every saloon between the two stations—at one of which I was treated to my first go-go dance (1940's version).

I am able to testify from this brief afternoon that Chicago deserved its reputation as the most servicemen-friendly city in the nation. And lest it appear that I am giving more attention to the travel than the visit, let me remind that it took a good half of two weeks to make a round-trip from Lincoln to Boston in those days of wartime rail transport!

All this came to an end—it seems not long after the return from Boston in the winter of '43—when the pressures on the Army (both political and logistic) to get those non-combatant students into the infantry could no longer be withstood. With very little ceremony—although with some little TriDelt wailing—we all were shipped off to infantry divisions, where we were to take our "specialized training" into combat.

More of this will be covered in essays yet to come, but I must be allowed one vivid memory. The Cadet Colonel of our ASTP Regiment at Nebraska was the very model of a soldier-student. Tall, fair-haired, with great military bearing, he stood at the front of our military formations as a prime example of young American manhood.

Early in 1945, when I had successfully withstood a heavy German barrage during the night, in a stone farmhouse in some French border village, I helped dig out the infantry unit in the house across the road. They had taken serious casualties. One of the dead we uncovered was our ex-Cadet Colonel, then just one more corporal who had given his life for our country . . .

ARMY III

At the end of our time at Nebraska, the war began to turn serious for me and my ASTP classmates. Our studies were broken off as were those of others at other schools in the program: for the best of American reasons, political pressures which could be wrapped in larger, more patriotic cloth.

The Army had been taking serious casualties. After the relatively quick Allied successes in North Africa and Sicily, the Germans had stiffened in southern Italy. The losses to ground troops there, plus the necessary buildup for the Normandy Invasion and its southern France complement, called for massive reinforcements in Europe.

The need for lots of infantry divisions caused the demise of the ASTP before its first classes had graduated. All of us were shipped to cadre units from National Guard or other reserve divisions. We were a relatively easy target, and there had been congressional attention to (understandable) cries from the parents of other youths in the service who had not been so visibly "lucky".

There were other consequences to all this, I am sure, but one of them was a heavy concentration of young college undergraduates on the front lines as combat soldiers—in roles they were never intended to fill—where they became statistics in the casualty lists far beyond what their numbers would have called for. I weep for those many who were less fortunate than I . . .

My road led me to the 44th Infantry Division (Co. G of the 71st Inf. Regt.) at that time (February 1944?) on maneuvers in the Louisiana woods. I don't recall departure or arrival on the train that carried us to maneuver areas near Natchitoches, in northwest Louisiana near the Red River.

But I do remember the culture shock at being deposited into an infantry unit in the middle of some woods far away from home and mother! We spent some weeks marching and maneuvering, but the only thing I specifically remember—besides the chiggers!—is having a Sunday dinner with some buddies in a ramshackle house, in a clearing in the woods, prepared by a nice Louisiana matron for one dollar a head.

It featured fried chicken (my first!) and yams and gravy and fresh rolls— didn't compare with our T-bones in Lincoln, but it sure was better than our wilderness Army chow. Beyond that, the next thing I remember is when we were making our way through some serious flooding on a train to Kansas.

We spent the next several months, spring and early summer, redoing basic and then advanced infantry training at Camp Phillips, outside a town called Salinas (not Salina), which I can no longer locate on the map. Maybe it disappeared when the infantry left. But I don't have a single image of the town, village, or hamlet of Salinas—just of the dusty camp town which was Camp Phillips.

While we were there I learned how a PFC (I had been promoted while in ASTP) earns his $54 a month as a rifleman in Kansas. There was a lot of marching and combat training under simulated and live firing. Like how to duck when your own artillery starts to shoot behind you instead of that nice, rolling barrage in front of you that had been promised.

There were chigger bites acquired during a goofing-off episode in the high Kansas grass. And there were buddies whose worth one got to measure as you went through the same exercises of body and spirit on the way toward being pronounced "combat ready".

The names, except for a few, have long since disappeared from memory. But the faces are still there. The 44th was made up of New Jersey and Pennsylvania blue-collar worker bees. Different from my Ivy League friends at Nebraska—but we all bled from the same shrapnel and bullets when it came to that.

My Sgt. was named SFC Adams. I remember him especially because he was the first combat casualty we had in France—if you don't count the First Lieutenant who shot himself on the eve of our first battle . . .

Anyway, Sgt. Adams cut his nose on his helmet when he dove to the ground to avoid our first air attack (from one of our own P-47 close support fighters)! He was a good man; I hope he made it through the war.

My pup tent mate (later my foxhole buddy) was a Pennsylvania Dutchman named Zimmer (?). We went through training and combat together, and we became so close that later, in France, I actually risked my own skin to rescue him from machine gun fire when we were out on two-man patrol together. But there was no one there to write us up, so there were no medals.

As I recall the outcome of that action, it was actually comical. When the last survivor of the German machine gun nest sought to escape, he and I ran into each other around a tree in some woods; when he dropped his rifle before I could drop mine, he became my prisoner.

As Zim (who had recovered) and I trudged along a railroad track back to our lines, we were met by our Assistant Division Commander who was on a one-man patrol (Brig. Gen. Walker—later captured in Korea while doing similar foolhardy stuff). The general allowed as how it shouldn't take two American infantrymen to deliver one prisoner of war (I think he mentioned that arithmetically we couldn't afford that kind of success), and one of us had to return to the unit. For the life of me, I cannot remember which one of us it was!

The last I saw or heard of my buddy Zimmer was during the Bulge in a bivouac in a snowy field near Saareinsmingen, after I had been transferred to the CIC. I don't know if he made it home . . .

At any rate, we plodded through our Kansas weeks and months until it came time to put all that training into practice. In Midsummer 1944 we set out on our way to what turned out to be Normandy. We shipped by train to Camp Miles Standish on the Cape in Massachusetts, a staging area for the convoy that was to take us to Europe.

Here I recall very well that the paymaster caught up to us with two month's pay on the day we arrived. We had all just been given three-day passes (our last!), and I spent the time between getting paid off and the departure of the bus to Boston in a little game of chance.

I had still not learned that Ivy Leaguers can't compete with native craftiness! By the time the bus rolled in, I had lost the whole two month's pay in a crap game. Fortunately, I had bought a round-trip bus ticket before the game started. (This experience was my next-to-last major gambling encounter. The last occurred in bivouac in Normandy, where I had a lucky streak at craps, won back all the monies I had previously lost, sent it all home and gave up the practice!)

That last visit home is a blur. I recall walking from downtown Lynn past the Newspaper office where I had worked, past the High School, along the route I had walked so many times, past friends' houses, through the Ames playground area, finally to our tenement on Boston Street.

The two days at home were filled, I think, with goodbyes to family and friends—those who were still at home: but this time with an edge of finality, since we all had the feeling that this might be it. Fortunately time has sealed off the details in some hidden corner of memory, perhaps never to be recalled.

Back to Camp Miles Standish, and the transfer from land to sea. We embarked from Boston Harbor (I think), and the whole 44th Division, 16,000-some strong, crammed into an Italian passenger liner (name famous but forgotten) for our trip across the Atlantic. We were to be part of a huge convoy (200-plus ships) which formed off Newfoundland and steamed away through calm mid-summer seas.

The ship had been fitted for transport duty, which in my case meant my own bunk in the sixth tier of hundreds of bunks in a cavernous hold.

Bits and pieces of the "cruise" come back: the words "blue tickets on the starboard side" meant "go to the right if you want chow".

After we left the sheltered coastal waters, chow became a problematic occasion. First heavy swells, later high wind-driven seas caused the steamy Mess areas to be dangerous both physically and nutritionally. If you could keep your plates and yourself from slipping and sliding across various wet metal surfaces while you ate, you then had to find your way to a railing to return it all to the sea!

Actually, I never did get to barf. I just felt miserable the whole voyage because I felt as if I had to. Unfortunately this trip (and its companion return voyage two years later) have given me a lifelong distaste for ocean cruises, much to the displeasure of other family members.

In mid-ocean, the ship was forced to heave to (speaking of barfing!), because one of the twin propeller drive shafts broke. The remainder of the convoy sailed on, leaving us with one lone destroyer escort circling us on sub patrol while we were dead in the water. This led to one of the truly unbelievable coincidences of my life!

Almost 25 years later, Betty and I entertained in our Munich home a German Navy Captain, a true gentleman named Winter, who was at that time the CO of the German Navy Comm Center at Flensburg.

While exchanging war stories he related some of his experiences as a U-boat commander on Atlantic patrol. Would you believe that he had been trailing our convoy (remembered the troopship's name and the date and the circumstances which made our 16,000 men a prime sitting duck), and that he had fired his last remaining torpedo a few days earlier!

Happy in our ignorance of all this at the time, the crew made repairs and headed after the rest of the convoy. Several days later (day 12?) we steamed around the southeast corner of England, right past the white chalk cliffs, and made our way to the battered port of Cherbourg in Normandy. And it was off to the War!

VIGNETTES FROM COMBAT DAYS-WWII (INFANTRY PERIOD)

The marching on of more than 60 years now has quietly eroded from memory most combat experiences, working along with the blessed ability of the mind to close down the more painful passages of life.

Further, my dutiful compliance with Army rules against keeping notes in combat—which I have later seen was more honored in the breach than in the observance—makes any really ordered recollection unlikely.

To try to preserve what remains, however, seems worth some effort. And there are things which I do want to write down, with every attempt to be as accurate as possible, as subject as they are to the vagaries of advancing years.

- I cannot forget even today the first dead body which I saw, even before we came on line. It was a German soldier, still unburied in the Norman hedgerows two months after the battles there. I remember noting his belt buckle with its "GottmitUns" inscription, and its implication that this would somehow help him elude the soldier's fate which alas! did catch up with him. (This was the first of many evidences I saw that God is neither with "us" nor with "them" in our temporal conflicts. I am sure we are left to our own devices, God forgive us . . .)
- Crowding upon that comes the picture of a Norman farmer as he, with the kindest of intentions I'm sure, introduced a few of us to the searing warmth of his home-distilled Calvados. The taste and acrid bouquet of that native "applejack" lingers on.

- Ending our few days in Normandy, a late-summer evening moved to a railhead at St. Mere Eglise (or was it Avranches?) where we jammed ourselves into some WW I 40&8 boxcars and slid down the tracks leading us toward our own "soldiers' fates".
- My first view of Paris: the freshly liberated cosmopolis looked pretty mundane when viewed from the railyards—with only a slight exaggeration I claim this, my first visit to that great city, was at "port arms".
- At the end of the rail line, somewhere in the area of Nancy, we de-trained and began a full field pack march toward a still moving Front. We marched and marched for at least a day (?), and took shelter in the haymow of a village barn. Over the years the splendid lassitude that overcame us in that soft bedding, under roof, has returned to mind many times when I have been tempted to fuss about a too hard mattress or "sub-standard" accommodations.
- Another day, another march, and we moved into a recently vacated (enemy?) bivouac in a wooded area, where the slit trenches and foxholes were almost ready for us to occupy—even to their own water supply, since all had been dug down through the local water table!
- The next evening rumor told us that we were to move into the front lines in the morning, replacing battle weary Seventh Army troops. I was dismayed and saddened to see how many of my comrades chose to spend their final evening before battle: standing in long lines waiting to visit two pup tents in which two women had chosen to sell themselves to "us liberators". (Rumor was that there was a duffel bag near the tents filling up with the proceeds).
- As we were taking position on the line came the first barrages from German artillery and mortars. Digging in involved deepening and improving holes which had been left by retreating German soldiers; we figured they knew where we were, so we dug deeper!
- Then there was the first patrol—in many ways the most nerve-racking of experiences, involving as it did moving out through mined fields in the dark, toward unknown opposition, to gain intelligence about where they might be and in what strength, and how to get through without blowing oneself to pieces by an incautious—or cautious, for that matter—step into the night. (I

have since learned that there are other ways to gather intelligence which are far more interesting and productive—although I share some of the atavistic skepticism of the combat commander about these other ways, since he must still send out his patrols in the end).

- In a quiet period between artillery barrages in another wooded hideaway, I remember the first, early snow as it dusted the trees and the boughs covering our slit-trench homes for the night. I was so moved by the sight that I slipped from hole to hole offering a small fir for sale as a "Christmas tree"—until the next incoming put an end to that tomfoolery.

- A Field Mass, celebrated in a barn at company "G" headquarters, and the truly moving experience of watching the uniformed priest raising the Sacrament as we kneeled in the hay.

- (Shortly after safely negotiating the open slope back to my own platoon, I stood erect preparing a K-ration on the "roof" of my slit-trench. A lone mortar shell exploded in the trees, and a piece of shrapnel slammed into the back of my neck, knocking me into the roof and the K-ration. I remain convinced to this day that my attendance at that Mass caused me to turn away in time to avoid catching the shrapnel full in the throat . . .)

- Another escape: after a 12-hour preparatory bombardment, my buddy and I failed to hear or see the signal to move out on attack until we saw our tanks moving up to our foxholes in what must've been a matter of minutes later. We hurried to catch up to our platoon-and did—where we learned that our places in the line had suffered a direct, mortal hit from German 88's.

- Later (days?hours?), as that same attack began to move slowly forward, our infantry column was halted in the dark by machine gun fire. My squad inched toward the point of fire, and I (for the first and only time in combat) pulled the pin from a hand grenade and prepared to throw it. Before I could, the German machine gunners surrendered to another squad, and I frantically recovered the pin and reinserted it with fumbling fingers, in the pitch dark! There were only three gunners, and they had bravely (from their country's point of view) held up a whole army for a while. In the morning, as we moved forward accompanied by tanks once again, I saw their broken bodies in the road. I did not know how they came to die in the night, nor do I now, for sure. But I feared then and now that it was one more example of how war, in its visceral terrors and angers, can make some men do awful things in the heat—or under the cover—of battle.

- The first encounter with the company Aid Station, where true heroes did their jobs incessantly, fighting to keep alive sparks of life until more sophisticated medical attention could be reached. One of the most vivid memories is of being a stretcher bearer for a wounded rifleman (actually a classmate from Nebraska) and watching as a corpsman at the aid station reached his hand deep into a wound in the soldier's back in an effort to keep him alive . . .

- In later phases of the battle, whose days seemed to run into weeks, our company moved routinely into harm's way and we took some heavy casualties. Elsewhere I have written of taking our first personal prisoner back to the rear, and of being pinned down again by some very personal machine gun fire. But we survived as a company even though seriously diminished in number.

- I've also written how we were relieved and sent back to serve as XVth Corps HQs guards. On the way I endured my final combat action as an infantry soldier, though there were others after I had gone into the CIC. This came just after we had experienced the great joy of our first bath in well over a month on line.

Our company moved in line through some mobile showers set up behind the lines. We walked into one end, stripped off all of our clothes and walked into heavenly hot water showers, walked out and received a complete new issue of clothes, from buff to boots. You cannot imagine how refreshed and renewed we felt as we reformed our lines and walked back toward our temporary assignment at Corps headquarters.

When what to our wondering eyes should appear but a German plane, heading toward our column! Without thinking, our march line dissolved as we all dived into the muddy ditches at either side of the road. Thus came a quick end to our spanking clean clothes.

The attacker turned out to be an observation plane, probably a FieselStorch, and represented no immediate danger; but no matter! Ground fire knocked it out of the sky a few miles away, and I am ashamed to say that many of us, hopping mad at being mud-covered so soon again, vented our rage by firing our M1's as it fell to the ground. In our defense, we were all aware that our rifle bullets would fall several thousand yard short, but still . . .

- German fighter-bombers had become fewer in number. Those that still existed were undoubtedly being saved for use against our bombers. Later in our advance into Germany we were, however, startled to see the first jet aircraft screaming overhead at what was then an enormous speed. They were the first of the ME-262's; lucky for us, they were too few and too late to do much more than scare the devil out of us on the ground.
- Back to the infantry—we had broken through the German defense lines in France, and were headed toward the Rhine, still some distance removed, and still before the Bulge. When we came up against the Siegfried Line (it may even have been part of the Maginot line, though I doubt it), the large caliber artillery in the bunkers gave us pause.

Some strategic thinkers at Division or Corps-level devised a plan by which we riflemen should attempt to detonate artillery shells still in their tubes by firing into their muzzles! Of course we were not yet cleared for the details of such brilliant planning, but it did occur to us that if we could get into the required positions to shoot down their muzzles, the artillery guns would have to be lined up pretty much with where we were at the time!

Fortunately, the scheme was overtaken by events which I cannot remember. One of them was probably our being taken off-line and put into Corps security detail; and the other was undoubtedly my assignment to the CIC. Both are reported on elsewhere.

- My first view of an Autobahn—after the fighting troops had withstood the Bulge attacks and broken through the last line of defense in the South on our way to the Rhine. It was a stunning piece of road building, running between heavily forested stretches in the Zweibruecken area. The clever Germans had painted the center lanes green to camouflage the fact that they were using the wide four-lane highway as a landing strip.

As we drove our jeeps past them, the abandoned planes still sat among the trees on either side of the Autobahn, mute testimony to the fact that their fuel was no more!

- One of the most striking visual memories . . . It must have been in the late winter of 1944, though it might of been earlier or later . . . is of a huge armada of US Flying Fortress bombers soaring north and east toward their targets. It was larger by far than similar squadrons we had seen before. The silver birds were painted starkly against a cruelly blue sky, hundreds upon hundreds of them. We must have been below a merge point where bomber groups from England joined their comrades from Italy. I recall estimating over 1000—later being told there were more than 1400! I was witness (unknowingly at the time) to probably the largest single force of bomber aircraft in the history of the world. One which will never again be seen, God willing.
- When we reached the Ludwigshafen-Mannheim bridge over the Rhine, and made an unopposed crossing (after the infantry had cleared the defenses out of the two cities!), we witnessed a candle-lit white flag procession down the Neckar from Heidelberg. The town fathers were surrendering the town to avoid any further damage to their historical trust.
- A blur of roads and villages to the Frankfurt area, and we began to follow the route of the Main River east toward Wurzburg. On the way we move through Aschaffenburg (and a little suburb named Mainaschaff, whose Nazi flag I liberated) and a town (Lampertsheim?) whose cigar factory had been ignited by artillery fire; its last service was to provide free a pungent after dinner smoke to all in the region.
- From there, south on the "Romantic Road" (sadly losing our Commander en route, as reported elsewhere). We came to the Division's last organized major battle as it fought to take the fiercely defended, historic city of Ulm—a center of Bavarian militarism . . . I recall wondering at the survival of the starkly beautiful spire of Ulm's cathedral, poking its way heavenward out of the sea of destruction surrounding it.

With Ulm in hand, the Division forced its way south across the Danube, against surprise opposition—which we learned was being mistakenly provided by Gen. deTassigny's French forces coming down the Danube from the other side!

At about this time our CIC detachment sent agents to interview the widow of Field Marshall Rommel, in her home just south of Ulm. I do not remember whether I was one of the emissaries, so I probably was not. I wish I had been there, or if I was, I wish I could remember the details.

Once across the Danube, our war was rapidly nearing its close. I remember the beauty of the southern Bavarian countryside and its villages and churches. There was little organized resistance, although an SS Mountain division was reportedly fighting a rear-guard action against our advance toward the Alps.

As we entered Austria the flood of reported Nazi refugees toward Switzerland increased, and the CIC workload did likewise (see the von Braun episode, reported elsewhere). The scenery was magnificent as we moved into the Alpine approaches, howevermuch the likelihood that it masked unknown dangers kept us from unalloyed enjoyment.

Bands of armed soldiers—some deserters, some just separated from their units, but most still armed—and the remaining SS Mountain troops made our passage through the FernPass into the mountains of Tirol kind of scary. But we made it, with or without the help of Austrian freedom fighters, alleged to be in the area.

The first week in May arrived and we moved into the Vorarlberg and to the last stop on our war's timetable—the picture-postcard town of Landeck on the Inn River.

The final wartime vignette, the celebration of V-E Day in a picturesque hotel in Landeck, will be forever obscured because of someone's discovery that afternoon of a trove of French champagne the Germans had carried all the way from Paris to Landeck—only to have it served as the nectar of our victory celebration. I must've had a great time.

In between these various remembered happenings—in particular those from my combat infantryman's time—stretched the deadly, day-to-day events which are coalesced into a mixture of mud and blood and noise and frightening silences and cold and clammy fear. I can testify to the fear and to the rest, but I cannot explain exactly what caused us to persist in going on.

I suppose part of it was that we accepted it as our duty to country and family; part of it was an unwillingness to let down in front of our buddies; part was being caught up in group actions in lethal contexts, where to fail would affect your buddy as well as yourself. And part of it was the belief that what we were fighting for was worth it.

But none of it, as far as I was concerned, had anything to do with the glory or romance or adventure of battle. There wasn't any glory nor any romance, and what passed for adventure was not enhanced by battle. Those who hold the contrary view: that organized mortal combat between groups of living, breathing men—sons, brothers, husbands, fathers, or whoever—is glorious, romantic adventure, or is some repeating evidence of grandeur throughout the history of man—as my unknowing antagonist George Patton did—are dangerously, grievously, at times almost criminally, wrong.

It is bad enough—no matter how necessary or justified it may be—to be forced by events to take up arms against an opponent who threatens your country and family, and to place your life in jeopardy to protect theirs. One can even make the case that indirect threats (such as those made by aggressors who may well later turned against our own country) are sufficient cause to turn to the violence of armed military action. But it should be at last resort, and never covered with the false flag of the glory of battle!

Jack Harney

ex-combat infantryman

FROM THE MUD TO THE MIRE: HOW AN INFANTRYMAN BECAME AN INTELLIGENCE OPERATIVE

Prologue

Years after leaving the combat soldier's world I was called to task by a Vice Chairman of the JCS. I had remarked in my resume for an NSA Pentagon job—impressed no doubt by surrounding senior military careerists—that my own military service was "limited" to WW II, where I had spent some time as a fighting PFC. The good General took serious issue with that portrayal, and called me to his office to let me know just how important he thought such service was.

In the light of today's love affair with Normandy and the rest of the Central European campaign, he must have been right. Yet as I relive the media accounts of truly heroic actions of those times, I am not too sure but what my "limited" does apply after all.

Notwithstanding all that, I send you a description of what it was like for a simple rifleman to move out of the grandeur (and the horror and the terror) of the front-line combat infantryman's world into the "safe" haven of rear-echelon intelligence. The description of what happened to that PFC in the late summer and fall of 1944 is as I remember it, unrefined by historical research or any other useful sources.

....

Before

The war began for the 44th Division, and for me, when we landed in Normandy. The invasion had some weeks ago moved off the beaches—we were in fact the first troops to debark in Cherbourg harbor—but it's debris of unburied enemy dead and the fresh litter of destroyed engines of war still befouled the hedgerows. We dug in and waited amidst the stark signs of war we had been preparing for, but one for which I was not yet nor ever would be <u>really</u> prepared.

Over the weeks and months which followed we entered into that world in ways I can no longer adequately describe. In what must have been the earliest Allied troop trains to move out from St. Mere Eglise we boarded hundreds of WWI-vintage 40&8 boxcars(quarante hommes ou huit chevaux). Across newly re-won territory of France we hurried as far as rails existed to meet the tiring prongs of 7th Army, advancing from the South.

After forced marches to complete the final leg of the journey, we relieved battle weary troops who had run up against a stiffening German defense in the Luneville area. The hand-off occurred under heavy German army fire, so accurate that we first learned here how the German 88's had earned their reputation as artillery piece snipers.

There following a short time (it seemed longer then!) of jockeying, patrolling, minor moves through mined fields, lethal advances and retreats against fixed defenses; we later learned these were the preparations for a thrust through Alsace-Lorraine toward the Rhine.

The tree-burst became a way of life—and death—and the flimsily covered slit trench was all the protection we could afford. Small refuge, I learned one day, as I took "cover" just before some shrapnel to the back of my neck knocked my face into a previously friendly K-Ration. I recovered.

As the days went on, the deadly 88's—everywhere it seemed—took their daily and nightly tolls of young infantrymen: some who had trudged with us from Louisiana and Kansas training fields, and some who, as replacements for earlier casualties, never made it through the last 100 yards to their final assignments.

In the last stages before our attack, some 36 battalions of our own artillery had massed on the 44th Division (or was it the XV Corps?) front. In a 12 hour barrage scripted from <u>All Quiet on the Western Front</u>, uncounted tons of steel screamed overhead. At 0800 the barrage stopped, and we infantrymen and tanks started. Three days (or so) later, we broke through the lines of defense and headed (we thought) toward Berlin.

Our prize was more like a little rail station several miles away. The attack continued. When we slowed once again, the remnants of our company were ordered into reserve, and some of us were given the life-saving task of guarding XV Corps Hqs at Saarbourg.

At Saarbourg on Thanksgiving day (which for us survivors of Co. G, 2nd Btln, 71st Inf. Rgt. was aptly named that year, as though through heavenly intervention) it seemed that all the stars in the ETO firmament had gathered. Generals Eisenhower, Bradley, Patch, Hodges, Patton, Alexander(?) et many al had apparently gathered to plan the next push. They were leaving the Officers Mess as we approached our Mess for a hot turkey dinner. For 50 yards or so, saluting was really worth the effort!

The next day, or the one thereafter, it was not. Gen. George Patton discovered an unbuttoned button on some hapless GI's jacket—mine, if the truth must be told—and shortly after that our company was ordered back to the front-line! I will always believe that my unrestrained button was the cause of our return.

Now those who have actually experienced it will confirm that a return to combat is far worse than coming under fire for the first time. You know how bad it is, for one thing; for another, you are seriously afraid that the luck which helped you come through the first round may have worn thin. At any rate, you are not a happy camper when it happens. On that day I began to understand why one of our First Lieutenants, who had seen action in China, felt compelled to put a bullet through his arm on the eve of our first (not his!) engagement. But when we rejoined our unit, there were two messages for me. In one, I learned I was next in line to become an assistant squad leader—a dubious honor indeed at that time, considering the rapidly recurring number of opportunities for that particular post.

The other—clearly supervening—ordered me to report to some arcane unit called Division Counter Intelligence Corps. I didn't know what it was, but it was at Division Hqs!!! In the calculus of combat exposure, that was roughly equivalent to Paris. And so I took up my rifle and I walked, for the second time apparently rescued from the immediacy of the front lines . . .

I was about to enter the intelligence world!

During

I found my way back somehow to the rear echelon of Division, and approached the housing of the 44th Div CIC. In the doorway I met a clone of myself, a teenaged PFC, clutching his rifle, stepping hesitantly out into the muddy street. But in contrast to the buoyant expectations I was feeling, my unknown comrade looked bewildered, woebegone, and very, very unhappy.

I asked if this was in fact the CIC place, and it was. I asked if he were assigned there, and he was not. Then he volunteered that he had been summoned "for an interview" as a linguist, that he had flunked "the test", and that he was "returning to his infantry company". No wonder! I shook his hand, wished him well—never to see him again—and, with much of the day's buoyancy leaking away, I entered the door which he had just exited.

There are longer versions of what happened next, but in brief I passed successfully through the promised gates and became CIC Special Agent Harney for the remainder of my combat days. The key to what we would today call that defining moment of my life was, as in so many other critical times, a matter of chance.

My examiners were two lieutenants in the French army on liaison duty with the CIC. "The test" was an interrogation of a local peasant, suspected of sabotage. The lieutenants did not deign to use their passable German on a French (Alsatian) suspect—who would not or could not speak French! They chose the alternative of my high school French and my first-year German in a kind of tri-lingual interrogation. Somehow we got through it, with the crucial element being my desperate recall of the phrase "he's got to go to the bathroom" in both French and German.

Of such is the stuff of survival!

For the remainder of my fighting war I was in a small, five-man detachment with 324th Regt. Hqs.—not quite Paris, as I was to find, but much superior to the foxholes of my earlier days. We spent our time helping to counter intelligence efforts against the Division—collecting enemy agents, turning some of them, re-turning a few who had been turned again by their original handlers; setting up friendly environments—and, frequently, collecting useful tactical intel through interrogations of prisoners and other sources.

In the process we tried to duck overt threats (those damned 88s again), and some covert ones (enemy counter-intelligence efforts). It was not as if we had really moved out of the combat zone, but I did, and do, recall with some shame how my occasional operational visits to company-level advance posts were as brief as I could make them. I guess I was mostly afraid that someone would try to hand me a rifle again!

I got used to sleeping under roofs, and to eating cooked food and wearing occasionally laundered officer's(!) uniforms (despite the widespread rumor that the CIC meant "the Corps of Indignant Corporals", we were accorded officer status); and the sporadic shot and shell which came our way seemed an acceptable ante to put on the table. I even got to turn in my M-1 for a snazzy 38 Cal revolver—which I did not fire in anger for the rest of the war!

Seventh Army tactical successes moved our detachment CP in due course into the grand hotel of the metropolis named Saargemund (Sarregemines) at Christmas time. One evening our two French liaison officers and detachment commander were at our situation map, debating the location of the front. My infantryman's ear suddenly heard the old German burp guns not far from the hotel, and I was able to announce with more agitation than pride that the <u>front</u> had found <u>us</u> before <u>we</u> found <u>it</u>.

Doing a fast bit of pre-shredder shredding, we loaded our jeeps and left the luxury of the hotel without bothering to check out. We had unwittingly begun to earn our Battle of the Bulge spurs. For the remainder of the Bulge, we participated as the left flank of 7th Army maintained its shoulder against attempted German advances.

The front began to move forward again in late winter. Our Division fought its way from France through Germany and Austria to the Swiss/Italian borders. CIC activities which had become routine began to be spiced with chases and captures of various special targets as they tried to flee advancing Allied forces.

We were just behind them for the most part, traveling south along the ironically titled Romantic Road. Otto Scorzeny, Mussolini's erstwhile guardian, was one target (we didn't find him); Fernand de Brinon (Vichy envoy to Berlin) was one of a considerable number we <u>did</u> catch. In the process we lost our detachment CO to opposing SS forces who captured and tortured him before he died, near Rothenburg.

As the nets of encirclement tightened, batches of other high ranking Army-SS, government, Nazi party, and collaborating officials were rounded up. Perhaps the most famous, and certainly the most useful of these was Werner von Braun, along with his V-2 Rocket team.

The new detachment commander and I took them in tow after a hair-raising incursion through enemy lines and out again, only to find them in the hands of (what else!) a US infantry company. After we had guided the group back through the lines to our CP, a very brief interrogation quickly showed that this fish was too big for our nets; wherefore we sent him off to help us get to the moon.

[An interesting Phoenician sidelight to this phase is that we failed to detect key members of General Gehlen's COMINT staff who had fled into the Tirol. Whether this was due to our total ignorance of signals intelligence matters at that time (which I maintain) or a more general incompetence, that particular omission has been the occasion for considerable ribbing from German veterans in more recent years.]

The final days of the war in Europe played out for us in Austria's Vorarlberg, in a corner where three nations' borders join their craggy Alpine peaks. It was there that Peace broke out, and those blasted 88's were silenced, and we had survived. The transition from the PFC infantry soldier to career intelligence operative was well and truly underway.

(How a hot warrior went on to become a cold warrior may follow in future chapters.)

After

In the final days of the war the division passed into Austria, and we made our way through the FernPass—the last defended passage we had to force—and on into the town of Imst. Our final trek was toward the magnificently sited town of Landeck in the Austrian Tirol.

Outside of Landeck ("the corner of countries", where Austria, Switzerland-Liechtenstein, and Italy come together) we met with the U.S. 10th Mountain Division at the Italian border, and our war was over.

By its official finish a few days later, 44th Div CIC was quartered in the Bezirkshauptmannschaft in Landeck. Our war's-end celebration was brief, albeit spectacularly memorable. We continued our clean-up work to round up the remainder of Nazi officials who had fled to the area.

Before we had finished with that, we faced the decision whether to remain with the 44th in its reassignment via the US to the Pacific, or to sign up for postwar duty with the CIC in the occupation force in Germany.

I, along with almost all of my comrades, chose to become an occupier, failing to see much use for German linguists in any invasion of Japan but anticipating just the opposite for riflemen. Reinforcing the decision, a set of orders arrived assigning us to the Seventh Army CIC Command.

Very quickly we moved to our new posting with the 970th CIC detachment in Schwaebisch-Gmuend, just east of Stuttgart. For the next six months our "clean dozen" of special agents there worked and lived a life at a level which for most of us would be unrivaled in our remaining years.

In those first weeks we got involved in military government activities and some CID functions. As had also been true during combat, the "real" Military Government units had some trouble getting organized and into place. The CIC filled some of the gap, doing whatever we thought the military government authorities would've done, had they been there.

This carried over into occupation time and was, of course, in addition to our primary counterintelligence responsibilities. As a result, I recall our being involved directly or indirectly in selecting and installing key local government officials—as we had done during combat situations in the name of security. With some success, I would note: when I returned to Schwaebisch-Gmuend 20-some years later I learned that the mayor appointed during our stay had gone on to serve in the post with distinction for more than 20 years.

This was a logical corollary to our primary post-war CIC project of sanitizing local institutions of existing Nazi and para-Nazi administrators. Logical in that those who were not locked up in the process were the only candidates at hand.

Despite Gen. Patton's reportedly almost subversive views on the subject, a great majority of the appointees did the job well without turning Germany into a Soviet satrapy. It is probably true, however, that a more intensive job of vetting might have avoided later security failures in postwar German governments.

With our CIC hats fully on, we got bloodily involved in putting down local Werwolf (Nazi resistance) operations. One grievous action seemed to break the back of the group (at least locally). And we successfully turned off those returning German military officers who wanted to mount an immediate attack (as they believed Patton was planning) with the US against the Soviets.

But as noted, the CIC's major postwar action was the roundup of Nazi and para-Nazi officials. The allies compiled a list of official Nazi Party positions whose occupants were subject to automatic arrest, interrogation, and possible imprisonment.

CIC investigations centered on follow-ups to the notorious "Fragebogen" (Questionnaires), which were a prerequisite for issuing Food Stamp-ration cards to the hungering populace. With a characteristically German approach, almost all filled out their questionnaires completely, including positions held in the Party and associated organizations.

After that, it was a matter of determining which ones to arrest, rounding them up, transporting them to a local lock-up (a gloomy old local fortress), and completing the interrogations. There the CIC departed, leaving the rest of the action to others.

While I am certain that we netted many of the desired big fish, I know also that the procedure caught at least as many "little-wigs": village activists whose rank had more to do with the number of cows they maintained that it did with their political philosophies. In the long run, however, it all proved to be a necessary cleansing, and, I hope, did more lasting good than harm.

Our CIC detachment was quick to take the lead in reestablishing local civilization—for example, we reopened the first brewery in the area, we reopened the first ice plant to ice down the results of our first action, and we located the first CO_2 bottles to enable the local inn (which just happened to be where we lived and worked) to put on draught the results of actions one and two.

We also caused the toy magnate (and jailed Nazi official) Herr Maerklin to reopen his toy factory—in an early, unofficial version of plea-bargaining—in time for the GIs to send home to their families electric trains for Christmas.

Not that it was all work: there were some fringe benefits. To begin with, we had augmented our motor pool of battle-weary jeeps by liberating a number of classy civilian vehicles from our bag of senior war-time captives. There was a Citroen limousine from deBrinon (Vichy French Ambassador), a BMW sports roadster (from von Braun?), and an Opel sedan from, I think, the Von Papen group. That helped ease the rigors of travel for some of our official, and other, movements.

There was also the matter of our private stables, maintained by an ex-Rittmeister of the Polish cavalry. It became our practice to ride out before breakfast and enjoy a stirrup-cup at a country inn before beginning one more strenuous day of ridding the area of yet another group of penitent Nazis.

Our office was sited in a local Gasthaus, where we also had our quarters. One of the two public rooms served as our work area; the other was used as our Mess. The innkeeper served us meals she prepared from our Army rations (plus an occasional cut of venison or rabbit) in ways the Army had never thought possible!

To help us recover from the rigors of the work week, we had requisitioned a weekend villa in the nearby town of Goeppingen. Yes, it had been, and became again later, the home of toy-manufacturer Maerklin. And not far away, the village swimming pool in Heubach was put at our disposal.

Early on there were new beginnings all around us. Before the end of that first summer the first productions of the Wuerttemberg Theater came to the Playhouse in Schwaebisch-Gmuend. I remember the "first night", when the curtain was held until we CIC'ers, being counted among the city "seniors", had made our entrance and were escorted to our seats of honor. Heady stuff for a 21-year-old . . .

The German view of the CIC in our area (and probably elsewhere in occupied Germany) was at the outset largely a product of fear. To begin with, we were the visible local arm of the conquering armies who had exacted an unconditional surrender from them.

Second, we were seen as "secret security Police", and as such the successors to some pretty fearsome characters in the National Socialist hierarchy. Finally, as the senior officials in town, we were owed the fear-based respect and obedience that had been a cornerstone of German culture for hundreds of years.

We were able to trade on those mindsets without, I hope, taking unfair advantage of them. Most of us were barely out of our teens, the product of an America which was, to us, based on a kind of amiability. Most of us did not hate, and all were looking toward finishing our military service and getting on with our lives.

It was not difficult to sense the change as the Germans' fear began to be leavened with a kind of respect and even fondness for their occupiers— even for us in the CIC.

I am convinced that this was a useful ingredient in the prescription for recovery. Mixed with their growing guilt at the devastations and atrocities they had brought upon Europe, and with a stubborn, almost relentless will to rebuild their shattered homeland, it helped the great majority of Germans to accept their present harsh conditions with some hope.

And, of course, the enormous goodwill and vision of the Marshall Plan later made it all come true.

Whatever the reason, toward the end of our service with the post-war CIC early in 1946 there were the glimmerings of a new day. The defeated Germans, with much support, were taking on the daunting tasks of re-creating a country—and this time getting it right.

In December, my life with the CIC neared its close as I was ordered to report to the 94th InfDiv—an infantry soldier once again—and to travel with them back to the US for discharge! The first leg, a hasty trip from Schwaebisch-Gmuend to Goeppingen in the season's first snow was marked by one more escape from death.

As I snaked DeBrinon's old Citroen through the dusky and snowy hills, I swerved to avoid hitting two aged women carrying their firewood along the road . . . the Citroen's front-wheel-drive enabled recovery from a skidding, 360° maneuver between two yawning drops into "lower Germany", and all was well again!

The order to return home was marred only slightly by the requirement to doff the pinks and greens, and other perks, of our assumed officer status and resume the position of a Tech Sgt. in an infantry platoon. (In the CIC, special agents wore no visible sign of rank, but were accorded officer status. I even undertook to grow a mustache to support this temporary fiction! The mustache disappeared along with the status).

The 94th was in barracks in Oberammergau when I reported, and I used some leave to spend Christmas Eve with the cast of the 1939? Passion Play. It was an exhilarating and moving experience. A fitting end to the cultural exposure I owed the CIC.

On New Year's Eve, on the other hand, I officially celebrated my return to the infantry. There was an impromptu fire (water)—fight with some closet-Nazis in an up-until-then undamaged bar in Garmisch.

That proved to be my last warlike engagement of WWII.

The Division returned to Normandy (how the Circle comes around !) and a steerage passage back to the US and Fort Dix, New Jersey. In a few short weeks Uncle Sam released me at Fort Devens to resume my interrupted life, whose continuation through war's end and the Good Lord had chosen to ensure through the instrument of Intelligence work.

970th CIC Detachment (author is at left end of back row)

POSTWAR I – RETURN TO CIVILIAN STATUS

At the end of January, 1946 I was shipped to Fort Devens to end my military career where it had begun, almost 3 years earlier. Needless to say, the end was more pleasant than the beginning. After several days of filling out forms and waiting in the ubiquitous lines, in early February I received my discharge (and the "ruptured duck" pin which accompanied it).

(That was to be my next to last time at Fort Devens. The real last time occurred 27 years later in 1973, when I returned to visit the Army Security Agency Training School. At that time I was the Commandant of the National Cryptologic School and the Director of Training of the Central Security Service Training System—of which the ASA School was a part. The difference in reception was remarkable . . . As a side-bar to the visit, I inspected a class in advanced Morse operator training, in the very same barracks where I had slept away my first night in the Army in 1943!)

Back to discharge day. I also received some checks for several hundreds of dollars which raised me to a level of monetary well-being I had never before enjoyed. I headed for Boston and home, stopping only to spend some of those dollars on the biggest feed of fried clams you can imagine.

After some time renewing ties with family and friends, I faced up to where to go with all this new-found freedom. I was not yet ready to rush back to Harvard—I was in fact too late to enroll regularly in the spring semester. So I joined the rolls of the 52—20 club—$20 a week for up to 52 weeks was a stipend awarded to all discharged World War II veterans to help in the transition.

Wartime had truly dispersed that old gang of mine. But old friends trickled back, and along with new friends helped make reentry pleasant. We played some golf, lots of baseball and softball, visited some dog tracks, and generally enjoyed ourselves. We even cruised about in search of the occasional female companionship. We were much better at softball!

In the summer time (or was it the following summer?) I worked as a laborer with my brother-in-law Arthur McCarthy, installing asphalt driveways and paving the occasional parking lot. It was hot, hard work (as described elsewhere in these meanderings), but it was great fun.

In the fall it was back to Harvard. I was able to enroll as a junior, with the credits earned during Army service. The G.I. Bill education benefits allowed me to relinquish my National Scholarship grant, and provided for full-time room and board. I moved back into Dunster House (F51), with a roommate named Kenny Falk—a Classics major whom I remember solely for having introduced me to the music of Buxtehude . . . by pointing out that "Buxtehude", repeated continuously, imitates the sound of a train moving over its tracks! Previous roommates Larry Hyde and Robert Warshaw had disappeared from my scope, while Ray Brown had married and moved off campus.

After a bit I changed roommates. Chuck McDonald and Phil Jefferson (and Joe Flynn?) and I moved into Dunster C41 for the duration. We spent a marvelous time together, with one of the greater marvels being that we all got our degrees. Unfortunately, we did not graduate together, because the war had chopped our lives into differently sized segments. But the good news was that it had not chopped them short . . .

Harvard had changed from prewar times. Most notable to me was the change in the House dining rooms, which had changed to cafeteria serving lines. The days of linen table cloths and student waiters at each table were no more.

There was a more heterogeneous character to the student population. Veterans seemed to dominate with their older, more traveled faces, and the number of "commoners" had seemed to increase. Many of the undergraduates brought their wives, and a few their children, to live off campus. And an aura of seriousness surrounded our proceedings.

The seriousness was well-founded, as it turned out. We had entered the atomic bomb era and were being followed into the nuclear war arsenal by an increasingly hostile Soviet Union. The growing threat of a final war began to wrap itself around us, and it fueled my own private anxieties for many years.

Interestingly, Harvard's President James Conant was one of the more sanguine of the in-the-know physicists' world. In the only direct conversation I ever had with him (I was sharing him with seven other Dunsterians at a President's Coffee), he allowed as how it would be 5-10 (?) years before the Soviets would be able to develop "a bomb". A month or so later the Soviets exploded that theory, and their first atomic weapon. (In President Conant's defense, he was not then aware of the Soviets' acquisition of nuclear bomb-making know-how through their devastating espionage successes).

But there was still time and plenty of occasion to have fun. Living in Dunster House afforded me the opportunity to play on the House team in just about every competitive sport. I even tried out for and practiced with the varsity baseball team in the indoor tryouts in the winter-spring of 1947. I was one of the two leading first-base candidates—in my own mind the better hitter and a competitive fielder—but I left the team for other pursuits (one of them being Betty MacDonald) which seemed more important to me at the time. More later.

Chuck Mac Donald and I developed a very close friendship which lasted until his untimely death in 1965. He was the ballcarrier and I was the blocker in most athletic pursuits, though I carried the ball in some others; but whatever we did, we enjoyed the years together. And his inestimable legacy to me will live on through the family that Betty and I have created together.

Oh, yes; there were also some studies. I had changed my major from Classical studies to Germanic Languages and Literature. The hands-on experience I had had during the war took care of any language problems, and I worked reasonably hard at the literature aspect.

I fought my way back from one of the two C's I got at Harvard (this one administered by my principal professor, Karl Vietor) and earned a "cum laude" the hard way. The details are uninspiring, but I am sometimes still, late at night, impressed at the feat.

In the midst of all this I met my future (and, thankfully current) bride. Roommate Chuck developed a sister Betty, who was studying to become a nurse at Mount Auburn Hospital, just up the Charles River from Dunster! At one Sunday evening supper at Dunster I saw her with another classmate and said aloud, "I'm going to marry that girl". Despite the fact that Betty to this day disputes the historical accuracy of that account, I did . . . and I did.

I won't take the time now to outline the course which ultimately led to the realization of that forecast—I will later—but it was a classic path of "true love", which ran about as smoothly as one is told to expect.

And then came graduation, in the spring of 1948. I can't remember anything about the ceremony, except that I seem to recall Gen. Marshall's address outlining the European recovery program (the Marshall Plan)—but since that took place at the 1947 commencement, it must have been two other guys!

At any rate, I <u>do</u> remember that my sister Dot bought me a suit so that I could graduate in some sort of style. And that's what I remember about Harvard—mostly.

Graduation brought a whole new set of concerns. Like what to do about the rest of my life. Sounds like another chapter is needed.Coming right up.

Boston University German Department - 1949

POSTWAR II – THE DIVERGING ROADS

With a degree under my arm it was time to look around for what comes next. I had already turned down, somewhat reluctantly, the Army's proposal to commission me as a 1st Lieutenant, <u>Regular</u> Army, in the postwar forces . . . as it turned out, they were the between war forces. I have occasionally wondered how life would have turned out if I had chosen the military career road. It would certainly have been different; and, given Korea, it might well have been shorter. But it is ironically almost a surety that I would never have graduated from the National War College!

In the event, however, I elected to look over some other options. The first thing was to consider the Harvard Business School. Some of my friends at Harvard were already there, and the likelihood of a fiscally comfortable career would be quite high. I checked to see if I would be accepted—I would have—but after briefly interviewing with some local businesses, I decided that the world of commerce, with its concentration on bottom lines and apparent neglect of the "real" issues, was probably not for me. Later experiences bring that decision into question, but I do not regret it.

My thought processes at the time were in hindsight sophomoric at best—and pretty arrogant—but they turned me away from the world of business. Next, I considered Harvard Law School; but even at that stage I thought I knew the Law was also not for me. Probably right—I would've tried to reform the whole institution, with predictable results. (Worse yet, I might even have been elected to Congress, thus becoming a part of what I have come to consider our country's major institutional problem!)

I should mention that at the time I was by way of being a crusader in the Don Quixote mold. I was naïve, convinced that there had to be a better world—after all, had we not just laid our lives on the line for the purpose of preserving it?—and I was probably insufferably high-minded in all the "cosmic" areas of life.

So I decided to head for high ground in the groves of Academe. Teaching was, in fact, the high school objective which I had carried on to Harvard. I thus signed up for Graduate School at Boston University, with a teaching fellowship award and my eyes set on a PhD in Germanic Languages and Literature, and a career at some shaded campus somewhere.

B.U. was for the first year a piece of cake; I had a graduate French class which I could handle with my high school French—upgraded by some wartime practice with the French people and Army; a fairly easy course in English Lit; and a couple of graduate courses in German Lit which I was able to ace with the help of lectures and papers from my undergraduate days.

The M.A. degree was acquired pretty routinely. After that, things became more demanding, academically and otherwise. What with the courses I was teaching to undergraduates, the tutoring I was doing after hours to graduates, some tough linguistics courses, and a whole bunch of extra-curricular athletics on and off the field it was becoming a pretty sporty course.

And then Betty came back!

Our path had been pretty rocky since that first sighting in Dunster House when I had determined she was to be my future. Although we did date a few times, and there was a definite spark there, there was also another guy. And he was running well ahead of me.

He and Betty got engaged, then disengaged, then engaged again. For details I would have to recommend Betty's memoirs, when she gets around to writing them. But mine can only say that it was a very discouraging time for me, and one of much cynicism and disengagement as far as long-term relationships were concerned.

But one day, to my immediate surprise and still continuing happiness, who did appear at the German Department's door but Betty MacDonald, as pretty as ever and much less engaged! It was downhill in effort and uphill in reward from then on.

We married shortly after I had completed my course work for the PhD, and had passed the grueling qualifying oral exams. All that was left (and still is) was writing my PhD dissertation. Betty had earlier passed her exams to become a Registered Nurse, and was at work completing her B.S in Nursing.

After a wonderful wedding and a brief honeymoon, we joined Betty's parents on a cross-country wedding trip (which deserves its own chapter). On our return, we faced a year or two of scraping by until I could get a reasonable teaching job, but we were ready to accept the challenge.

Then came, almost immediately, the unexpected challenge of our first pregnancy. John, Jr. was on the way! Plan A was in danger, and we had no Plan B! We were living with Father and Mother Mac, who had affably taken us into their cramped apartment while we were getting our start, but none of us had planned on such a quick beginning.

I began to look for full-time teaching jobs, in the seller's market of 1951. Among a number of subsistence level offers at various prep schools, the best prospect was a job in the Boston school system. I applied and passed the necessary exams, but no immediate offer ensued; (later, after we had moved to Washington, I got an offer to teach at Boys' Latin, but it had come—fortunately—too late).

Then I stumbled fortuitously upon a radio announcement that a recruiter from the DOD's Armed Forces Security Agency in Washington was in town, looking for linguists!

Within a few days I had been interviewed and tested by a distinguished gentleman named Paul Hartstall, and a week or so later I received an offer of government employment as a GS-7, promising a munificent $4205 per annum—in the 1952 Salary Schedule.

I had to make a decision then and there. As it happened, the B.U. German Department announced its promotions that same day: the job of Associate Professor (to which I might have aspired after completing my PhD dissertation and about six years of work as an Instructor/ Assistant Professor) was quoted at $4200 even, five dollars a year less than Uncle Sam was offering Right Then!

It was clearly off to Washington, DC for us, and an unknown new career of unexpected breadth and richness. The details of the beginning of that life, including the rough start of leaving a growingly more pregnant wife to await the signal to come join me, are to follow.

Betty and Jack in their 1946 Ford—1951

POSTWAR III – OFF TO THE HALLS OF MIRRORS

On Christmas afternoon of 1951, after visiting with my parents in Lynn, I left to Betty in the full bloom of her approaching motherhood to set off for our new life in Washington, DC. As tough as it was on both of us for me to leave her, it was necessary to go on ahead alone to make the necessary preparations: little things, like confirming that I had a job, learning where I was to work, finding an apartment and some furnishings, and other minor stuff like that. And Betty and I wanted her to be with her mother when the baby came.

I rode off with Tom Boland, my closest hometown friend, in his car to an overnight stay in New York. We started out in a snowstorm which grew wilder as we progressed through Worcester and into Connecticut. Tom's skillful driving saved us more than once from minor accidents, and once from a major one.

We arrived safely, however, at his modest East Side apartment, where I spent the night. When Tom dropped me off at the bus station for Washington next day and I waved goodbye to him, little did we know that would be the last significant time I would ever see him.

(This is but one example of a major character flaw, which has led me throughout the years to concentrate so much attention to matters of the present and the immediate future that I have ignored those of the past—and as a sad consequence have left un-revisited many earlier friends and places, to my sorrow and shame . . .)

After a first night in Washington—staying within a block of the White House, at the YMCA—I reported next day to AFSA, the Armed Forces Security Agency, at Arlington Hall Station. It was December 27, 1951.

I recall standing in a short line outside the front gates to AHS (I <u>think</u> that was the first day) in a heavy overcoat—probably my Army-issue coat. It must have been the warmest December day on record, I guess in the mid-80s, and I know I got an altogether erroneous view of Washington winter weather on that day.

In a whirlwind of actions in the next days I was processed through the Pentagon and into the AFSA training school at 14th and U Streets, NW in Washington. I also found lodging with another AFSA-recruit, Joe Rogers, with a family on Park Road, in the 1500 block—a pretty, tree-lined street which has suffered serious physical and social decay since those times.

Joe and I shared a bedroom in the apartment of a fine family whose name now escapes me, a husband and wife and late-teens daughter (about to be?) married to young Marine. I stayed there through the six weeks of U Street training and into the first month or so of my assignment at Arlington Hall. Until I brought Betty and infant son John back to our Falls Church home. More of that later.

The Training School at U Street was a useful introduction into this brand-new, secret world I was entering. There was instruction in who and what the AFSA was, some general indoctrination into civilian federal service, and some specific training in cryptography/cryptanalysis/radio ops on basic, not very classified levels (if indeed they were classified at all).

It was all very interesting to me, representing as it did a segment of intelligence whose existence I had not even suspected until then. The six weeks also served to allow completion of a basic, top-secret level clearance investigation. This, together with successful navigation of a polygraph (lie-detector) exam was enough to proceed with formal indoctrination into the arcane world of Special Intelligence.

At this point, I was moved to my first operational assignment at Arlington Hall . . . [From here on, expect constraints in all work-related segments, owing to continuing security requirements which we, as opposed to all other forms of the media, will attempt to honor].

AFSA was an Agency of the Department of Defense. It was an early attempt to centralize the cryptologic efforts of the United States— which had been developed and conducted as discrete Army and Navy operations during WWII. It was headed by a feisty Army Brig. Gen., Ralph J Canine, who, I later read, had served as one of George Patton's many chiefs of staff.

AFSA was not successful in its attempts to bring Army (and the newly minted Air Force) and Navy COMINT under the Department of Defense, largely because of the compromises which had to be made to satisfy the individual Services. Whatever successes it did achieve were due largely to the foresight and personality of Gen Canine, who carried them over to the follow-on NSA. But those are other stories.

At any rate . . . With a newly minted badge hanging from my neck, attesting to my newly proven loyalties and trustworthiness (sort of like the medal awarded to the Cowardly Lion in The Wizard of Oz), I became privy to this strange new world. From the moment that day in mid-February 1952 when I entered the office of the Division Chief of AFSA-23 (Dr. Carl P. Klitzke) until the day in February 1980 when I walked out of my office on NSA's Ft. Meade Headquarters Ninth Floor, I was privileged to serve our country in ways I had never dreamed of. Even now I cannot see how I could have ever wanted a better career.

But I jump too quickly to conclusions.

While this beginning was happening to me, Betty was preparing us for another beginning with the birth of son John. That happy event occurred on March 4, 1952 in Brockton, Massachusetts, not too long after that week's Milton Berle TV show. Betty's father, James P (Mac) MacDonald, did the honors, getting Betty from their home in East Bridgewater to the hospital in Brockton in time. John, Jr. was born that same evening, as I walked around the Park Road neighborhood in NW Washington.

There was a lot of to'ing and fro'ing on my part as I traveled (by midnight bus, generally—conserving funds as was our wont) back and forth to East Bridgewater every other weekend. The trip was an overnight ride, but never boring, filled as it was with anticipation of another reunion with my young wife, and latterly, our son.

I recall one trip which brought me as far as Boston, depositing me in the results of a heavy snowstorm, in an area which had been further immobilized by a transportation strike. I made my painful way to East Bridgewater by a series of hitchhike rides from kind motorists of the day. I fear if I were to try that today I would be in for a very long walk indeed!

On the third trip or so after John's arrival, Betty and I drove back to Washington (our car had wintered in East Bridgewater) without infant John, to spend a few days getting our one bedroom apartment in Culmore (Falls Church) ready to move into. It was very difficult for Betty, but she took it all like a trooper.

Two weeks later we packed all our worldly goods, and baby John and all his worldly goods—which exceeded ours at the time—into our 1946 Ford sedan and set off with all the energy and enthusiasm of youth on a new life together into an uncertain future. The trip from New England to Virginia is one we'll never forget. It began an adventure we are still experiencing together. More follows.

THE VIRGINIA YEARS

From spring 1952 until the summer of 1957 we built our family and our careers from a home base in Falls Church, VA., living in the Culmore Apartments. We moved in as a threesome, and expanded to a fivesome before we left.

Culmore was a brand new garden apartment complex at that time, one of many which had been and were being built in the Washington metropolitan area to accommodate the growth of postwar government. It was located in what had recently been "country", but which had begun the enormous changes which have culminated in the Tyson's I and II (and . . .) culture and the development of the Dulles corridor and the Beltway and the I-95/I-66 growth zones.

But in those days we lived in quiet suburban surroundings near an undeveloped Bailey's Crossroads and a country drive away from a Tyson's Corner which still consisted only of a small country store and intersecting dirt roads. It was a time when our most ambitious Sunday drive could get us lost on a one lane road through the woods, looking for the alleged site of a new airport-to-be—Dulles—way out west.

Our early lives concentrated on the care and feeding of son John and the usually fruitless attempt to get a night's sleep to prepare us for the next round of care and feeding. Most of this, of course, fell to Betty, although I was involved to some degree while the infant stabilized into the baby.

During Betty's day she joined a number of young mothers in the same state of family building as we were. We made many friends in that circle and joined in communal ventures which helped in part to make up for the absence of extended families. We did not appreciate then how much

we missed the family support network, left back in Massachusetts, until we saw how it could work as our children began their own families.

Betty's mother (Grammie Mac) was available in times of real need, when the whole family became sick for example, and did on those occasions come to stay with us in Falls Church. More frequently she and Grampy Mac took Betty and the children into their home (in Brockton, Massachusetts, or in their summer camp on Martha's Vineyard) when I was sent away on temporary duty, or when Betty was just overwhelmed and needed a break. Even then, Betty had the primary responsibility for care and feeding, and it was not an easy time for her—it is to her great credit that she made it through despite all that!

In short order, at about two year intervals, we twice added to the family. First in 1954, Mary Ellen (Pi) came to join us, choosing to appear while Betty was staying with her folks on Martha's Vineyard. Two years later, in 1956, Kathy arrived in Arlington, Va., where her mother was at the time.

John and Pi and Kathy, with Betty and me, made for a good-sized family, and, as it turned out, a great group to be a part of. Pi's appearance led to a move across the street to a two-bedroom apartment, and Kathy's got us out looking for a three-bedroom house in pretty short order.

I am not the one to describe adequately either the joys or the difficulties of managing the family as it developed in those days—only Betty can do that. Perhaps in _her_ memoirs she will do so. What I _can_ say is that in those early, tough years and throughout the ones that followed she was the heart and soul and engine of our family group, as indeed she continues to be. And its successes are hers.

While the family grew through the Virginia years, I was trying to grow into the duties of my job.

My first assignment was to a section led by Ellie Carman, which had recently been spun off from Ann Harrington Skiff's section. There I met the first group of capable AFSA/NSA civilian colleagues, with many of whom I spent my career: Dave Youmans, Hal Jaeger, Bob Barrett,

Walter Wall, Alice Keosian, Swen Larsen and many others whose names no longer come as readily to mind.

Ellie put me to work as a clerk to help me get familiarized with things like raw traffic (intercepted communications sent in by our intercept stations) and many of the clerical processes it needed to be put through before being subjected to analysis by my betters. It was all a bit of a comedown for a Harvard graduate who had been teaching at a university a few months before, but it was a time to swallow hard and learn.

I recall making a pact with a co-worker named John Vogelpuhl, in the same situation, that we would just try to be the best damn' clerks in the agency. We began to compete to see who could turn out the most work in a day's time—with the result that it was not too many days before we were moved to more substantive assignments.

We didn't appreciate it at the time, but our Branch was unique in the Agency in that it had direct contact with and/or responsibilities for all of the functional parts of the COMINT mission. Accordingly my colleagues and I were able to learn about the whole spectrum of our business while we were still at modest section level.

My job title named me a cryptolinguist. Although one meaning of that would be "secret linguist"—which in fact I was—it really meant that I was a linguist whose job was to try to solve and exploit encrypted messages.

In those early days, however, I could not even refer to my job title outside the office, not to mention what it might mean as far as my duties were concerned! It made for problems in outside life, like getting credit from department stores or opening bank accounts. You could not tell people what you did or where you worked. The drill was to say you were employed by "the Defense Department". Fortunately, this had been going on long enough that the major stores could respond, "Oh, you work at Arlington Hall"; and when you didn't deny it, business could continue.

This concern with security—even if sometimes driven beyond the limits of good sense—was an admirable hallmark of the Agency throughout my career. What we were able to produce to the benefit of our nation and its people was considerable, at times even beyond price. The costs of protecting it were worth paying.

Success in cryptologic operations is in large part hostage to the ability to keep the "fact of" success secret. Thus production of this good is constantly at risk of being diminished or even denied through breaches in security.

There is constant pressure to "tell the story". In recent years NSA has chosen to give in to the urge. Perhaps correctly so. But I remain convinced that we needed in those earlier years to measure the public's right to know against our responsibilities to help it to survive. In that critical analysis, I believe we conscientiously made the hard choices and kept quiet. But then, what do I know! As far as I <u>do</u> know, the Agency did its job with great integrity and did not abuse the great powers it possessed.

Back to the ball game. In these early years (1951-1957/59) NSA began to do what was required to centralize direction of the nation's cryptologic operations. Replacing AFSA in 1952, the National Security Agency was established at the direction of President Harry Truman, and it set out at once on what was to be a far more successful course to become a "national" manager.

Among the actions involved was the concentrated effort to decentralize some of its operations to military units, while retaining necessary technical controls over how the job was done. The sine qua non of this was to get and remain on top of the job. I got involved in the early steps to this, and somehow was placed on the fast track. Promotions came regularly (even though I still had to work overtime and on weekends to make ends meet) and I moved into supervisory positions quickly, in fact faster than I felt qualified for.

In one move I was appointed "Monitor"—immediately referred to as the "Green Lizard" by my colleagues—over the activities of NSA in concert with a productive albeit troublesome field operation. The job required that I go to Germany on several TDY's—one of them over a period of months—at a time which was not conducive to my meeting family responsibilities. Whatever, a combination of technical success and Irish chutzpah on those occasions seemed to form a foundation for future advances in the profession. I do wish it might have been done with a little less turbulence . . . and a lot less extra work for Betty.

As we approached the end of our years in Virginia ('56), we had completed our family (with the birth of Kathy), and had about reached the point where we could think about taking on the challenges of a mortgage. I had been advanced to the level of GS-12 (some $11,000.00-plus per annum) and a Section Chief's job. (My section had grown to the 50-60 person level).

Then I was ordered to move with the Agency to NSA's new home at Ft. Meade in Maryland. Thus came the end of the Virginia years and the opening of a new Chapter.

THE MARYLAND YEARS (PART I)

Shortly before it became certain that we were to leave our NSA site at Arlington Hall for a new building at Fort Meade, it also became certain that the Harneys needed more living space. New home construction was beginning to erupt almost everywhere around the area, so finding a likely house was no problem. Finding one we could afford was quite another.

When a new development advertised three-bedroom homes in West Vienna Woods at $13,000, we hurried to see what they looked like. They looked like $13,000 houses; so on that Sunday afternoon we put down a $500 deposit on a $15,000 one. (It's surprising how little emotion that $500-figure would arouse today—at that point it represented a very large part of our net worth!).

This turned out to be the first of several investments I made which over time have convinced me that the market is just not meant for me! It is not that it wasn't worth the money—in fact, that house is worth much more than $400,000 today. But I got cold feet by Monday morning and backed out of the deal later that day.

At just about that time we were told that we would all be moving to Ft. Meade, and our search for a house turned toward exotic places like Cheverly and "Georgia Avenue extended". Most family Sunday afternoons (Saturdays were still consumed by that blessed overtime) were occupied by getting the three children into the car (by that time a two-door Ford) and making whatever rounds we could before we, the children, or the car gave out.

Finances limited our choice to those whose down payment we could afford—thank the good Lord and a benevolent Congress for the VA five-percent down, 4 1/2 percent mortgage! After wearing ourselves and the car down we located and settled on our home in New Carrollton, in whose modest den I even now write down these occasionally immodest words.

We have lived here on and off for more than 50 years—successfully warding off all blandishment to enrich ourselves by participating in the cyclical real estate booms during those years. The family had two overseas tours—whose details may interest or bore you in later chapters—a tour at the National War College, and two tours at the Pentagon. All of these provided ample opportunity and some reason to move out of our New Carrollton house into upgraded environments.

In each case the children resisted any further moves—naturally enough, since Carrollton was the ground into which their early roots had caught hold. When these feelings were added to my own inertia, there was always sufficient rationalization for us to stay put. And if truth will out, the overriding demands on my time and attention from ever new assignments kept me from any meaningful pursuit of newer housing. After the children, and their reasons, moved on, the press of years and the continuing generations provided their own reasons to stay put. But we might have done worse.

In the early New Carrollton years we became involved in the building of the community. The major attraction of New Carrollton was the promise—largely fulfilled—of participating in a kind of old fashioned town-meeting-driven kind of community government.

Participate we did: as president of the Civic Association, secretary of the incipient New Carrollton Pool, and in various other associated community activities. In the process we made many friends. Those of longest duration are the Hixsons. We had met Gene and Mary as across-the-hall apartment neighbors in Falls Church, parted when they moved to Indiana and we to Germany, and reunited again in New Carrollton from 1963 on. They are as close to family as any we have in the Washington area.

Speaking of Germany, when I was selected to take a posting to the NSA European field office in Frankfurt, our Maryland Part I years came to an end. The end was not final, but the momentum we had established with and among the community movers and shakers had dissipated by our four-year absence abroad. It was not to be reachieved.

GERMANY I – THE FRANKFURT YEARS (PART 1)

The road to Germany began, unbeknownst to me, with my first assignment in AFSA. I had been recruited because of my background in German, so it should come as neither a surprise nor a security violation to note that my early jobs had to do with German and our European operations.

The early TDY's made from Arlington Hall were directed at European operations, with our German sites central to them. My various assignments in the Atlantic Division of AFSA and its successor organizations in the new NSA were all significantly involved in the creation and management of field operations in Europe.

As I was promoted into supervisory line jobs (from deputy section chief to section chief to deputy branch chief by early '59), more and more of the work was taken up by actions to decentralize to military field sites some of the things we had always done at headquarters. This was an important element in the creation of the world-wide SIGINT system, which it was to become my privilege in later years to help direct.

It became clear early on that a tour in Europe was in the direct line of career progression for me. I didn't know exactly how important it would be, but I recognized the need to experience field operations from the field, and able to see the growing headquarters—field station—field customer interrelationships from the field perspective as well as from that of headquarters.

Visits from the field had decided me to turn my sights toward the operations officer job at NSA Europe in Frankfurt. It was clearly where the action was in those days. While I was still too junior for that post (by two grades in '57, when I started to think of overseas possibilities), I felt no urgency to rush to an early assignment.

Then events took hand. Benson K. (Buff) Buffham, then Chief NSAEur, came back in early '59 on his mid-tour recruiting trip and offered me a job in Frankfurt. When I told him my intent to wait until I could qualify as the Ops officer, he said, "Don't wait too long, who knows when the train will pull out!" or words to that effect. But I demurred, and he headed elsewhere.

At about that time, Betty's folks came by to visit with us, and her father talked me into taking a week's trip to Florida with him, where he might see a horse race or two and I could enjoy the warm breezes. In brief, we were gone for about eight days. And on our return, I found I had been signed up for an assignment to Germany!

Ann Carachristi, my "big boss" of those days, recognizing the importance of such an assignment to my career, had taken it on herself to volunteer me for the job Buff had offered. And so the deed was done. By that action, Ann became one of the several important sponsors in my years at NSA, and made it possible for Buff to become another, perhaps the most important of all.

From there it was off to Germany. Much of the late winter and spring of '59 was taken up by preparing ourselves—the family, the house, friends and relatives—for a major dislocation.

The journey began when Betty packed up the children and I packed the car (a two-door Ford Victoria coupe!) for the day-long drive to Brockton, MA, where we were to spend some time with Betty's folks and to visit mine in Lynn, before we left the country.

We enjoyed the brief time we spent in our home territory. The visit was marred by John getting hit by a swing (a number of stitches to his head which were to be removed by a German doctor in Frankfurt!), and by a dead rabbit—signifying a fourth child on the way (which turned out to be a false alarm, but only after a very anxious few weeks in Germany).

We had left from our New Carrollton home with empty pockets, owing to the expenses of settling on the house and buying necessary furnishings, etc. so that we could move in. As a matter of fact, we had to sell our car in order to get out of the red—the first, and thanks be, the only time to date we have gotten in over our heads in our married life. Betty's father was the lifesaver, arranging to have the car sold and sending us the few hundreds of dollars after our arrival in Europe, allowing us to dig our way to even, and to get on with things there.

This stage culminated in the flight from New York to Frankfurt, via Newfoundland and London, which deposited us in a strange land in the midst of strangers for the next four years.

Author receiving a commendation from Mr.
Buffham as Col. Hill looks on -1960

GERMANY I – THE FRANKFURT YEARS (PART II)

We arrived at Rhein-Main airport after a long, tiring flight on a prop driven Lockheed Constellation (at about 15,000 feet, one had not yet achieved the wonders of the seven hour crossing, high above the turbulence of these earlier times). The children (John 7, Pi 5, and Kathy 3) took it all very well, though Kathy showed a certain amount of childish pride at recounting to our fellow passengers the number of times she "frew up". As for Betty and me, we survived.

The next weeks were a combination of confusion and anguish, most of the latter accruing to Betty. She had a hard job of adjusting to various sets of temporary quarters, in the process learning about U.S. Army military housing regulations as interpreted by mostly unsympathetic local nationals.

Our first quarters were on the fourth floor, no elevator, of an area called Lo-Cog (Hi-Cog being a much nicer housing area, but at that time well above my pay grade). While I got to go off to work each day, Betty had the job of entertaining three rambunctious kids while learning how to live in a military community. My most vivid memory of those early days was when Betty and I were conversing with our sponsors (Dave and Rosie Youmans) in the street below, John Jr. was standing at an open window four or five stories above us. He didn't jump, but my heart did.

Betty had to cope with the job of moving from those temporary quarters to another set of "permanent" (they lasted less than a year) digs, while I was off on TDY to Nuernburg. She still trembles at the memory of scrubbing up the apartment, alone and still believing she was pregnant, to satisfy an implacable German housing inspector who had to pass on the apartment before we could move out.

In between, she got the older children (John and Pi) into the Army school at Frankfurt, and arranged for some help with Kathy until she could join them in the following year. Just to help fill out her days (and nights!) the children began at that time their four year battles with smoggy Frankfurt's endemic respiratory diseases (all the childhood staples, plus a few others).

It was a good thing we were still young, although in retrospect, I still can't understand how Betty pulled us through it all. But we coped, and gradually moved on to more pleasant memories from the Frankfurt times.

Meanwhile, at the office, I was learning my way into a new job. It was a combination of back-room cryptanalysis on a very spooky set of problems, and a growing amount of special project activity. Special projects meaning those things which didn't fit into the standard technical support and organizational/representational functions which made up most of the NSA Europe agenda.

One of the first odd jobs I was given was the one which took me to Nuernburg while Betty faced the task of moving us to newer quarters. I had to locate and engage a German lawyer to represent the family of an employee who had been killed in an accident in Germany while on temporary duty from the Agency. Ironically, the employee had come from my old branch, and I had signed off on the orders which had sent him on his fatal trip.

Other, less emotionally draining tasks began to fill my days. A growing NSAEur involvement with NATO affairs soon required much attention, and I became active in liaison matters on the international level; that led soon enough to some contacts with officers from other NATO members' national forces. And that led in turn to involvement with in-country CIA "coordinators". It was a most interesting and educational time, one which was to prove central to my later years in more senior jobs in the Agency.

Most of the first two years were a mix between operations (providing tech support to various field stations and my "behind the green door" cryptolinguistic duties) and a growing list of staff officer functions. I began a series of operational visits which led me to London, Paris, Cheltenham, Heidelberg, and most of our field stations and headquarters in Germany. In the process I gained invaluable working access to the collection and field analysis and reporting aspects of our business, and, equally important, began to meet and listen to the principal field customers of our product.

Then the liaison functions took over full time. As the U.S. began to work more substantively within the NATO context, improved intelligence interactions with SHAPE partners (including the U.K. and Germany) came under review. I became a junior part of a senior study group which investigated various improvements.

In short order I was called on to use my abilities in French and German. I was able to serve as an interpreter in a series of conferences (including meetings chaired by General Gehlan, first president of the BND, and one for the CG of the U.S. Army V Corps and his subordinate CENTAG German commanders, my first and only experience with UN style simultaneous interpreting).

But language was even more important in one-on-one contacts with foreign officers where accurate understanding of what was being discussed was all important.

The details are no longer of any import, but these early contacts with a developing international security apparatus shaped significantly the paths my later years took in the intelligence community.

The Frankfurt job required much travel back and forth to the States. One trip involved a four week working visit at Fort Meade, where the DOD's Combined Group Germany was conceived and fleshed out. As one result of the trip, I was appointed to the post of U.S. Deputy Chief of the Group, which was originally housed in NSA Europe's Frankfurt spaces.

Speaking of housing, we had moved from our third floor Lo-Cog apartment to a duplex house (which my then GS-13 rank called for) in the U.S. Army housing area in Bad Vilbel outside of Frankfurt. In less than a year, after another promotion, the Army moved us into a full house in Bad Vilbel, where we finished our Frankfurt tour two years later.

Promotions were important at any time, but had more visible impact in an overseas assignment. DOD bureaucratic rules called for civilians to be treated, for some things, in accordance with their "equivalent" military ranks. Although it was the source of some resentment on the part of some of the "true" military, this extended into housing and other protocol governed matters.

NSA had, during the two years before we left for Frankfurt and in the first two years we were there, been under a four year freeze on promotions. Fortunately I had been promoted on the last list prior to the freeze, and on the first one after it ended. Partly due to the latter, we became a two car family in Bad Vilbel, as we bought a new ('62) VW bug.

My stay in the Deputy CGG job was relatively brief, although full of excitement. Among other things, it involved working with the Army and the local CIA'ers to locate, finance, and prepare acceptably secure working spaces in Munich. With Madison Mitchell, CGG's first chief, I beat a path between Frankfurt and Munich on every kind of conveyance short of dog sleds. And we always arranged for our arrivals in Munich to coincide with the official opening of Happy Hour! CGG relocated to Munich (without me) in March 1963.

In the final half year of the Frankfurt time I finally achieved my wish to become Operations Officer of NSAEUR. Bob Drake's tour was curtailed, so that he could prepare to attend the National War College, and I finished our tour in that coveted job.

[I just missed out on having it during the Cuban Missile Crisis, but in all honesty, I and the rest of us were fortunate that Bob Drake was the Ops Officer at that point. I learned a great deal about handling myself under pressure by watching Bob run Operations during that critical period.]

This first overseas assignment was critical to whatever success I achieved in my career with NSA. Perhaps the most valuable aspect of being overseas was how it thrust one into situations of responsibility and authority far beyond those which confronted colleagues of similar experience and grade levels back at Headquarters.

Take the matter of releasing messages (which is what we called sending official telegrams). Back at NSA Headquarters I had barely reached the level where I could release messages on purely technical matters. But if they involved policy, or operational control, or interaction with customers, I was at the bottom of a long ladder. Numerous staff and line officials would have to concur (i.e., review and edit) before some higher authority would release the message for transmission.

It could literally take weeks before any sort of controversial subject could be raised or responded to by official message. On the other hand, in the field there was neither the time nor wealth of staff to allow this. I was amazed at the latitude of responsibility and authority I assumed just by virtue of being away from Headquarters.

Overseas assignments like mine were great experience accelerators. There is no doubt but that the increased responsibilities and the requirement (and the latitude) to grow up fast served as a springboard to senior jobs for almost all of us. We were able to see the Agency from the outside, as its other field components and their customers do, and still operate as a part of the inside.

Another value of the overseas assignment was that most of the Agency's senior managers (and many in the DOD and CIA) came to the field on visits. We in the field offices got to meet with them on favorable terms: they were away from their home turf, they needed our help to survive on ours, and they got to see us perform close up and personal, both in the office and on the road.

Last but not least of the field assignment bennies, were the strong personal and professional ties we developed with our cell mates at the office. Many of us came at a critical grade level, GS-11, 12, or 13. We were relatively young and medium junior. Professionally we were still learning, and still teachable. In the small office we could be cross trained in various disciplines by each other. And we learned to respect and admire our colleagues.

The time of this '59 to '63 tour embraced some of the most dangerous happenings in the Cold War, certainly after those the country survived in the Korean War. There was the Cuban Missile Crisis, undoubtedly the moment of greatest peril, and repeated saber rattling over Berlin.

We tested each other by pushing the intelligence collection envelope (remember the U-2's), and ran up and down the border looking at each other in belligerent poses that might have led to serious mistakes. But it was a "good" time to exercise the system, and we learned from it.

While this was going on in and away from the office, Betty had to manage the burdens of the household. With three children (3, 5,and 7, ripening during this tour to 7, 9,and 11), you would think she would have her hands full.

And she did. Just contending with childhood sicknesses, guiding the children through their early school years, and keeping them on track would have been a full time job even in a familiar environment, with a support net of family and friends.

But that wasn't the way it was. She had to cope with the Army, with the Germans in the German economy and in the Army system, with a husband who was (a) on TDY, or (b) calling her at 4:30 pm from the office with a fresh load of visitors who "were coming by the house" for a drink, or for dinner, or to see the town, etc., and she was without access to home and mother.

How Betty (and some of her counterparts) did it all is remarkable, and that she did it with such good results is even more so. Our being thrown in together with other Agency families of comparable age and family situations was helpful, even though it added to the social workload, and the ties we all developed in the "Frankfurt Ghetto" have lasted through the years.

Finally, in between all the above, there was some opportunity for rest and recreation. We were able to travel as a family to some places we might otherwise not have seen: to Italy, Switzerland, Austria, Paris, Holland, England and other places in Germany. I regret very much that the demands of my particular job, and the timing of them, sounded so loud in my ears that I did not take better advantage of these years for the family. But we can't do it over again, and what we did get to do together in the Frankfurt years has become an important part of our lives, in many ways.

The Harney Family circa 1963.

Betty with son John Jr and daughters Mary Ellen and Kathleen in
Bad Vilbel (Frankfurt) at Mary Ellen's First Communion—1962

THE MARYLAND YEARS (PART II)

A sort of nightmarish return to the U.S. put an end to the Frankfurt experience. Packing out of quarters and loading ourselves and our three children and our twenty-three (?) pieces of luggage onto another plane was only the beginning.

After another low altitude flight back across the Atlantic (it was still only 1963) we arrived in the pre-dawn hour in New Jersey. With our semi-awake children (by now grown to 11, 9, and 7) we crammed onto an overfilled bus and rode through the darkness up to New York City, John and I standing all the way.

In New York we transferred to two taxis, one for the luggage, and headed off for the Port of New York where we found (Praise be!) our Opel wagon, released it from customs bondage, and set off down the New Jersey Turnpike for home. Apart from a piece of luggage flying from the roof in a heavy rain and heavy traffic, followed by a visit to a New Jersey filling station to get a minor (but critical) part replaced, we came safely back to Maryland.

[I should note that overseas travel for the Agency in those years was quite burdensome for those with young families and limited budgets. In part due to the efforts of those of us who suffered through those earlier times, the process later became far more tolerable. It also became more irritating for me to listen to the crowing of those who, in later years, profited from our PCS travel experiences!

I should also note that it was not all the government's fault. Part of the blame was due to our (my) own inexperience with how to make the system, such as it was, work for you, and part to our (my) desire to get on with the demands of the new assignments waiting as quickly as possible. That caused me to choose air travel rather than surface (ocean liner). This is one of the things I would certainly do differently, given the chance to go that route again.]

Back in New Carrollton, we began to put the house and ourselves back together. We had rented to some Navy bachelors who proved to be good tenants (one of them went on from his Ensign status at that time to become a Rear Admiral, in charge of Naval Intelligence). Except for the dog. But that's a relatively small matter, when looked at in the sweep of time.

We installed central air conditioning, put in carpeting through much of the house, and settled in for a stay. It was one of the several times we should have moved to a new house, but inertia, the travails of the recent moves while overseas, the return, and the desires of the children to resume their lives in old surroundings (kids are always like that), gave us reason enough to stay put.

Back at work I was put in charge of the organization in which I had been the Deputy four years earlier. A branch then, inflation in the interim had upgraded it to Division status. Despite the added honor, however, I was not very pleased. It seemed to me that I had grown considerably in the four years overseas, and I was more than ready to move on.

I guess, in retrospect, that I made my feelings all too clear, an Irish trait I'm afraid, and as a result neither I nor my fellow workers benefited, especially the next level higher staff people. My disgruntlement was directed primarily at them for presuming, if you can imagine, to help me to do a better job!

In short order I was called on a high-level carpet, which at the time covered the floor of Mr. Buffham. Letting me know that my demeanor was helping no one, especially me, Mr. Buffham told me to calm down and to stay put in the job, that I had been put in for a promotion, and that there were other possibilities not too far down the road. I calmed down on the spot.

Yet it was a bit late, at that. I began to have the blood pressure problems in those post-Frankfurt days which were to be my lot from then on. Nonetheless, the promotion was almost immediately made (to GS-15, a very satisfying level), and within a few weeks thereafter I was moved up to the Chief of Staff job at Group.

This was a major jump, two levels higher than where I had been, and put me at once on "mahogany row". In those days only the very senior jobs (probably well under 100 in number in the whole Agency) rated wooden desks and leather armchairs, and there I was in one of them.

[Ironically, within a month my chronic back pains, first contracted 18 months earlier in Frankfurt, made it impossible for me to sit in any comfort in my luxurious throne, and I had to replace it with a hard-backed secretary's chair! Thus I experienced my first real encounter with professional hubris. Would that it had been also my last.]

The Group's Chief of Staff job was a bit more than an honor. As it turned out, there was no staff when I arrived. The first task was to assemble one and get it working. The second was to meet the challenges to the integrity of the Group, and its Chief, an honorable, capable, likeable man named Frank Austin.

Mr. Austin had good reason to believe his effectiveness was being threatened by some of the worrisome, though in retrospect well meaning, free-ranging actions of his principal subordinate Office Chiefs. That was in fact the reason he chose to appoint a strengthened staff in the first place.

But it came a bit too late. The barn had already been emptied. The stresses of that period took a serious physical toll on Mr. Austin, who was carried out on a stretcher not too long after I arrived, pure circumstance I still claim! But he did not stay for very long after his return. He was reassigned to a less stressful job (as Commandant of the National Cryptologic School) after a short while, where he, and the school, prospered.

During my relatively brief stay in that job I got to witness the beginning of the long path to the end of the Vietnamese morass, the Gulf of Tonkin incidents and their aftermath. My group included the Agency offices which had the con in that part of the world.

I was well removed from the actions of that fateful Tonkin Gulf night, although I was on duty and in the formal chain of responsibility. But there was no time for formalities or chains then. It was real-time action and reaction both in the field in South East Asia, and at Headquarters at Fort Meade, directly between those who were in the gulf and those here trying to help them make sense out of what was happening, right now!

In the sweet thereafter, I was also not directly involved, being sent off to school and to other assignments. Thus I missed the broadsides that were fired at all the "Gulf of Tonkin" parties, and the investigations and who-shot-John's over why our military involvement in Vietnam was ratcheted up so abruptly.

All I can offer now, to the best of my memory and knowledge, the events of that night were professionally analyzed and reported in that night as quickly and accurately as the intel community's considerable abilities allowed. What other higher-level actions followed, or what other opinions of the engagements were achieved in cooler, post-action studies, does not alter my opinion as to those first responses.

Later on, when I discussed the Tonkin incidents with an anguished colleague at the War College, the Captain of one of the two USN destroyers on the scene, we could only commiserate with one another. Security excluded our other classmates from the discussion.

You can imagine how I appreciated his descriptions of the roiling seas, the darkness, and the urgency to respond immediately to the perceived threat to his command, and how much he needed, and appreciated, the support of a participant even as far removed as I had been. As always, truth is in the eye of the beholder.

Before he left, Mr. Austin had given me an unknown, but greatly appreciated and most important honor, the nomination to attend the National War College as the NSA member of the class. (In the early years of the NWC, NSA had only one slot each year. In fact I was to be the last of that breed. Beginning the year following mine, NSA was not to have fewer than two members in any NWC class). It was an important step toward the highest level of Agency management.

The War College year (Class of '66) was an outstanding experience. Its beginning, however, was marred by a far more important event, the death of Betty's brother and my friend Chuck MacDonald.

Chuck had moved his teaching job from eastern New England to the West Coast some years before we went off to Germany. He had met and married his wife Lynn, and they and their twin children Scott and Laurie had happily ensconced themselves in a nice home in La Jolla. Chuck was successfully engaged in high school education, and by 1965 had been appointed principal of a modern regional high school then under construction, due to open in the next year.

While we were overseas, Chuck had begun treatment for a malignant melanoma. His condition gradually worsened and, after several operations, had become terminal by Spring 1965. Betty and I flew to California to be with him and his family in his final days at the City of Hope Hospital. It was a traumatic experience for Betty, but she played out her role as the stalwart support of the family, waiting until our return home to submit to her own grief.

It was not a happy beginning to our year at Fort McNair. Yet life went on, and we became involved in the extraordinary experience of being a National War College family. More on that to follow.

Author being congratulated by Dr. Tordella after notification
of appointment to attend the National War College -1965

THE NATIONAL WAR COLLEGE AND THE PENTAGON (PART I)

The year we spent at the National War College was yet another of the defining times in our lives. The class was about 125 or so, relatively equally distributed among the Army, Navy-Marines, Air Force, and various civilian agencies (including Coast Guard). As said earlier, NSA had one slot (in later years expanded to two or three) which I was appointed to for the '65-'66 school year.

The curriculum was centered around national security affairs, and intended to give the students an understanding in depth of the components integral to the "national security": the DOD and the armed services, industry, the press, the executive branch and its congressional overseers, State Dept, the intelligence community, some other cats and dogs of the national government, and a fairly healthy segment on international friends and foes.

Course matter was presented largely in lecture and discussion format, supplemented by readings and selected optional courses, and topped off by a thesis-like Individual Research Paper which each student was required to prepare, submit, and defend in an oral presentation to his (in those days there were not yet any "her") classmates. My IRP was on NATO—more I cannot remember without a trip to the fearful attic storage area!—for which I received a "Distinguished" grade in my oral defense, but nothing special for the report itself. It must have been eminently forgettable if even I don't remember it . . .

There were field trips (to various military bases for live and static demo's, to the U.N. to see it in action) highlighted by the Spring Overseas

Trip, in which five groups of students visited separately each of five key overseas areas: Europe, the Middle East, Africa, the Far East, and Latin America. The "gentleman's trip" was reputed to be the Latin American junket. I was a member of that one.

It was to be my only trip to that part of the world, at least at government expense. Stops at the Panama Canal Zone, Caracas, Brasilia, Rio de Janeiro, Asuncion (Paraguay), Buenos Aires, Santiago, Lima, Guatemala City, and Mexico City: all instructive, all memorable; but details will have to be covered elsewhere.

General impressions were that the whole area was in serious social and political disequilibrium because of the unrelenting distances between haves and have-not's. The visits' concentration on the military controllers of much of the area was, though understandable, disquieting. The trip would doubtless have been of great, specific value if I had ever been given any special responsibilities for that area, which I was not.

The War College had much to offer. Probably foremost was the opportunity it gave each of us to associate with one another. To begin with, the class was made up of unusually well qualified people (I must depart from my usual modesty here, but only in the interests of accuracy!).

Students were selected from among those in each service or department who were expected to move onward and upward. Selection was an indicator (though not quite a guarantee) that you were on the short list for consideration for flag/general officer, or its various equivalents in the civilian government hierarchy.

Roughly half of the military officer-students (who all arrived either as colonels/Navy-CG captains or selected for promotion to that rank during the year) subsequently were to go on to flag/general rank; civilian class members virtually all made it to supergrade or equivalent levels; in fact several civilians in our class had already made it before arriving at the school.

The value of that, apart from increase in pay and privilege, was that NWC graduates acquired both a general bonding to many of the most senior members of the government security and foreign service establishments—graduates from previous class years—and a more specific, close tie to their own classmates. In the years after graduation, the NWC-generated common experience encouraged interaction among leaders in the business, which grew in importance as class members advanced to more and more senior positions.

In the longer term, perhaps more important bonds of friendship grew out of the NWC year and the years of professional involvement which followed. Our own class, NWC-66, has been having periodic reunions which continue, even after forty years and counting, the warmth and friendships of those times.

The academic year itself gave a series of valuable insights into how the national security apparatus of the nation worked. Coming as it did while the country was so deeply involved in the southeast Asian destructiveness, 1966 was a year in which insights were at premium value.

The Class was divided among Hawks and Doves (by no means equally!); I was a member of the Doves, if only because I could see no useful purpose to our measured expenditures of blood and treasure, and I was unwilling to go to the extreme some of my "let's stone-age 'em" classmates espoused. (Interestingly, if not surprisingly, students from CIA were among the most stridently bloodthirsty).

Despite these differences, the class was united on the overriding purpose of the nation, even in those days of division, and even given Vietnam. With the common desire to help our country meet its national and global goal, we could focus on the long ranges, and we did not let ourselves be swallowed by the maw of the moment. It was remarkable. I continue to be proud of us.

Just one more word about the Vietnam divisions; Betty was a Dove without wings! That is to say, she felt strongly that what was going on about Vietnam was wrong, and that the country should withdraw immediately. But she did not feel it would be proper to voice her sentiments, given my job and position.

She noted that the U.S. was without any real friends in this—only bought and paid for allies were supportive. And she was more sensitive to the ravages caused by real divisions in the country than most of us were.

And yet she did not feel she could express these views in any but the most private settings <u>because she did not want to endanger My Career</u>. While I thought I understood the differences in our opinions—I believed them more in form than in substance—I did not sense how deeply she was torn by the situation. If I had, I would not only <u>not</u> have been against her speaking out, I would have wanted her to. I just did not get it.

How sad that was. And how sad for your husband to be an active part in something you felt so deeply was mistaken almost to the point of evil. Unfortunately, we did not talk it out at the time. Where we did discuss it, we must have talked past one another. It occasionally happens, even in the best of families . . .

....

When the NWC course ended, I began my year of penance. As was customary for those NSA'ers who had whiled away a gracious year at Fort McNair, I was sentenced to spend the following twelve months in the Pentagon.

It wasn't really all bad. In those days the NSA representation consisted of an NSA rep to the JCS (a Navy Captain), and a very small staff. That office's deputy chief (the most recent NWC graduate) was dual hatted into the OSD office responsible for NSA affairs, where he (always a "he" in those unenlightened days!) served as an integrated staff member, working primarily on program-budget matters.

So far, so good. As the deputy NSA Rep and the only one with access to both the JCS (nominally) and the OSD (actually), I was called on to sit at the table for the weekly Director's Staff Meeting. This was my first entree into the rarified "Ninth Floor" atmosphere, as a semi-senior. [The "Ninth Floor", housing the Director and his staffs, was used as the shorthand for NSA Senior Management.] I thus had my first routine experience with the top brass in action.

I was somewhat star-struck at those early ninth-floor staff meetings; the director (Gen. Marshall "Pat" Carter) was impressive, being a very articulate, quick-witted man, with a live sense of humor. His off-the-cuff exhortations to all to play on the same team were just what I thought the doctor should order. It came as no little personal disappointment to see there was little follow-up to the words, and that his obvious (to me) abilities to lead were largely unused. I guess his priorities lay elsewhere.

One of the bad parts of this first Pentagon tour was the propensity of the Director and some of his staff to try to use the incumbent as a direct line into the Secretary of Defense. It didn't work and was the source of some embarrassment, both to me and the Agency.

For example, on several occasions I received letters from the Director addressed to the Secretary, with instructions to deliver them "directly". Most often the letters centered on criticism of the office in OSD where I worked as an integrated subordinate with my other hat on, and embodied some request or other which would have bypassed that office.

Now I, as a GS-15, had little direct access to the SecDef. (I would have thought that our director, with his wide experience in the military bureaucracy, would have understood that). Consequently, I would deliver the letter to the Sec's military assistant, a Major General; it was his job to get correspondence staffed before dropping it on SecDef's desk. As a result, the letter often beat me back to my OSD Office, where the chief (my other boss) was likely already drafting a reply for SecDef's signature. The fact that the letter was in criticism of the OSD office in the first place just made it all the more laughable.

As it happened, the "boss" was a likeable Irishman who was so steeped in the ways of Pentagon Bureaucracy that he saw nothing very strange about all this, and didn't take it out on me personally. Nonetheless, I found that to be a hell of a poor way to run a railroad, and I did what I could to change it. But that's another chapter.

For the remainder of the Pentagon Tour No. One, I spent the majority of my time working on the OSD response to the NSA Program-Budget. I am not known as a numbers man, but I did the best I could. I <u>was</u> able to help our Pentagon masters better understand the mission sense behind the dollar figures, which helped make up for the occasional arithmetic boo-boo.

Except for one! The Pentagon was at the time (actually, at all the times) interested in keeping the bottom line at or below the politically acceptable Figure of the Year (1967) long since surpassed, perhaps by a factor of three or four, for all I know. After we had all done our magic, we were still over by about $68 million. A trifling figure even then, but politically touchy.

Again and again we re-did <u>my</u> figures—all were fairly sure that's where the error was most likely to be found. No one could solve it. We even brought in outside help—no luck. Then I, in desperation, looked at the next year's program: there the error had grown to $69 mill. The light went on! When the following year showed a $70 mill overage, the problem was solved: I had been adding the fiscal years (which I had placed at the top of each column) in with the dollar totals. I was really embarrassed, although in retrospect it took a linguist's imagination to find the mistake . . .

[Sometime during the year (or was it later? Can't remember) I was asked to appear before a group at NSA which was looking at organizational matters. Walter Deeley was on the committee, but I don't recall the others. At any rate, I raised the issue of NSA representation in the Pentagon, and argued that it should be changed.

My proposal was that we should establish an NSA office in the Pentagon, man it with a staff knowledgeable on the JCS-OSD matters, appoint a senior, well-known NSA Civilian as its head, and act like a first class outfit, instead of an outgrowth of some other OSD office.

As I recall, I recommended that the Agency wait until there was a general change in the OSD (after an election), when such a reorganization would be lost in the other noise. Little did I know that exactly that would happen in a few years, nor that I would be one of the senior NSA civilians to be assigned to that post!]

My year in the barrel crept on, highlighted by the '67 Arab-Israeli war, and low-lighted by the Israeli felony against the Liberty (?). There were frequent occasions to work with OSD/International Security Affairs, where NWC contacts were helpful, and some general working of the E-Ring.

But all in all, the best part of that experience was that it led directly to the Munich assignment. Which follows.

GERMANY II – THE MUNICH EXPERIENCE (BEGINNING)

In the last months of the Pentagon tour in the Spring of '67, I was asked to consider going back to Germany. I had, as you may remember, spent a good part to the Frankfurt years in special liaison work. That included assignments involving NATO, DOD contacts with the CIA in NATO.

In the course of that experience, I had participated in the design and establishment of the CGG. Now, in 1967, I was being considered to become its chief. But there was a problem of timing. The chief's job was not to become open until 1968, which, for personal reasons, would not meet our family requirements.

Betty and I had long agreed that we would time our moves from place to place so that each child could finish high school with at least the last two years at one school. If we were to begin a three year tour in '68, that would mean Mary Ellen (Pi) would not be able to do that, since she would be spending the first two years at Munich American High School and returning to Maryland for her senior year.

The Agency and I found a compromise: we would go for the first year in '67 as Deputy Chief, and I would move up to the chief's position for the final two years. Thus Mary Ellen (Pi) could have her last two years in the New Carrollton school after our return, graduating with her class in 1972. John would have all three years at the Munich American High School, and Kathy would begin high school after our return. Naively, I thought that would solve the problem.

So, it was off to Munich in late summer of '67.

Once again I hurried the family's move, since I felt I was needed in the new job RIGHT NOW. We had spent a week or so in Massachusetts during the Christmas break, where the children could visit with Grammie and Grampy MacDonald and with their Grandmother Harney. They also got to meet with their cousins on both sides of the family. It was the last time they were to be with their Grammie Harney.

In late July, early August, we left from Dulles International Airport on a flight to London. There we moved into what had to be the tiniest hotel apartment in all of England, and spent three or four days bumping up against one another, and doing the tourist things one does in London. (I still can't remember whether or not we gave in to the children's urging to "do" Carnaby Street. I hope we did, but I fear I didn't).

From London we flew to Munich via Frankfurt's Rhein-Main Airport. I recall that our Frankfurt-Munich flight was in first-class, a happy accident that aroused a hunger we have not often been able to assuage.

We were met by the Youmans, whom we were to replace for the second time (we had replaced them in Frankfurt on our first tour. In the interim, Dave and Rosie had come back to Frankfurt, on their way to Munich, where they replaced us in the Deputy Chief CGG job. A kind of ingrown personnel policy, wouldn't you think!).

In Munich we were assigned a relatively sumptuous, five bedroom temporary apartment at McGraw Kaserne—the VIP suite normally used for brief overnight stays by TDY'ers. But our search for appropriate permanent quarters went on for a while, and our temporary stay lasted for at least five weeks. As it played out, I was the problem.

Before I left Washington, I had been promoted to GS-16, a supergrade rank. Since this qualified us for general officer quarters, we posed an embarrassment to the local housing officer, who had no "real" generals to house, but had only one or two general officer houses to let. Dr. Klitzke (the current CGG Chief, also a GS-16) was already occupying one, at the sub-post in Dachau, and the other was being held in reserve in hopes that a REAL general would arrive soon.

The Army solution was to move Dr. Klitzke to a posh requisitioned house in Gruenwald—across the street from the still famous movie star Senta Berger—and to move us into Dachau. The Klitzkes moved, but I simply refused: the quarters in Dachau had been the residence of the infamous Concentration Camp's commandant during WWII. In addition to my distaste at having any personal connection to the horrors of those days, I did not feel it at all appropriate to use that house to entertain foreign visitors, officially or otherwise.

As a result, we had to stay put in our temporary quarters for some five or six weeks. Ultimately the local Army authorities saw fit (in part, I am convinced, as a result of some steamy cables I sent off to the Army Headquarters at Heidelberg) to upgrade one of the twelve colonels' houses in PerlacherForst to general officers status, and to move us into it. More to come . . .

But it was not to be all that simple. While we were awaiting the Army's response to my messages, we received one from the Director, NSA, ordering us to move to Frankfurt forthwith, to replace the Chief of the NSA Europe office—who was being removed before his time, with some haste.

Believing, as I did, that I would be of far more use to the Agency as Chief (ultimately) of CGG than as Chief of NSAEUR in Frankfurt. I tried (in two separate messages to the Director) to talk him out of this move. I failed. Consequently, Betty and I headed for Frankfurt where we met my new "command"; we arranged–without problem–for a general officer house, set up with the local Army schools to accept our children, and prepared to move into the new posting.

On our return to Munich, we spent the evening with the Klitzkes (more about this splendid couple later), who were entertaining a senior NSA visitor, Mr. Frank Raven, a true technical great in the NSA pantheon. He had been the key NSA figure in some international discussions in which I had played a part. Frank listened to the story, agreed with our contention that I could do us more good in Munich, and got the Director to reverse his decision. THEN we moved into PerlacherForst.

Thus, somewhat controversially, began the tour which was to highlight my operational career and to make possible my move into the upper levels of NSA management a few years later.

[In case you have noted, this whole tour so far seems to be about housing. That was not the case, of course, but the care and feeding of our overseas population, including housing, was critical to our being able to accomplish the missions we were assigned. And in the case of representational jobs, which this one certainly was, appropriate settings for official entertainment were a prime requirement.]

The Combined Group Germany was tasked with a number of classified functions which are still prohibited by law from public disclosure. We will not discuss them in any ways which would violate this prohibition. However, those aspects which ARE in the public domain should suffice to give some understanding of the context in which this very interesting part of our lives took place.

CGG had a bi-national staff. The Chief was an American, with a U.S. Deputy and a U.K. Deputy. Staffing was largely U.S.; a few U.K. nationals were also assigned. Under NATO procedures, both U.S. and U.K people were treated alike when it came to support (cars, feeding, housing, etc.).

[Time for another sidebar. NSA was established as an Agency within the Department of Defense, but it had a NATIONAL mission. (That's a story in itself, but not for here.) While we had an active-duty military officer as our Director, we were largely a civilian agency; there were military folks assigned, including a few senior officers, but almost all top-ranking jobs were held by civilians.]

There were some tensions as a result of that mix, but by and large we got on quite well together. In the overseas environment, however, civilian-military tensions often led to problems. Almost everywhere overseas, NSA's people lived and operated in a military world. All support we received – office space, family housing, medical care, schooling for children, churches, gas for cars, access to commissaries and PX's and clubs and recreational areas, etc., etc.—all was provided by and through local military commands.

You would think we civilians would have been properly grateful. But no, in many cases we were really quite the opposite. We complained about housing and rules and the requirement to show identity cards and the quality of the benefits we were given and the lack of "freedoms". It was all too human and all too understandable—but it led to misunderstandings and increased tensions.

And then there was the matter of rank: always a problem in the egalitarian civilian world. But when NSA civilians were exported overseas, the DOD regulations required that they be assigned "equivalent" ranks. Starting with GS-7, all civilians were given officer status/comparability: from 2nd Lt. on up through general officer equivalencies for the supergrades (GS-16,17, and 18).

Now that raised tensions on a large part of the local military, in particular where it came to housing. Virtually all the people NSA sent overseas in those days were relatively senior, which created instant competition between military officers and senior civilians for premium quarters.

In the larger posts, the relatively high grades of DOD civilians could be absorbed, since there were relatively few of us. In the smaller posts, there were larger problems. Munich was one of the smaller posts. In addition, we had the complication of having U.K. civilians on our roster: THAT called for military equivalencies twice removed!

Thus it was absolutely essential that the senior officials in the various NSA/DOD postings, CGG in particular, "get on well" with the senior military people locally. Munich stuck us with a number of opportunities to come unglued in the support area. That I was able to pilot the CGG successfully through those shoals I will always consider as one of my better accomplishments. Appropriately it was accomplished with great help from Air Force Major Paul Cummings, who was the pilot for the pilot!

When we finally moved into our quarters on "Colonels' Row" on BantingStrasse in PerlacherForst, there was tinder ready for igniting. We had been well identified as intelligence folks, already one strike against the visiting team, and our refusal to take the house in Dachau had forced the Army to put us in Perlacher, thus reducing by one the single home quarters available for colonels.

Shortly after we moved in, one of the colonels invited us to a block party at his quarters. When we came through the front door, a bit late, a palpable hush set in; Betty and I both felt we were in for a baptism by fire. You were almost sure they had been discussing what cover story THIS pair will try to pass off on us. So as we walked into the living room where all waited, I blurted out "Hello, we're Jack and Betty Harney, the new spooks in town!"

For some reason it worked, and the ice began melting perceptibly. Betty and I are most grateful to the artillery officer, now long since dead, who hosted the party and helped us to confront the problem head on. It was the commencement of a comfortable set of relationships. And of our three year tour in Munich.

Shortly after this beginning, CGG was faced with a problem of housing for the large family of a junior linguist arriving from the States. There were about nine children, as I recall, and counting! The largest apartments available had a max of four bedrooms, and these units were at a premium.

Major Cummings worked with the Army and prevailed on them to knock out the walls between a three and a four bedroom unit, thus providing a generous solution for burdensome problem. Paul was a magical worker.

Our final housing issue involved the Harney family once again. In Perlacher, there was one real set of general officer quarters, unoccupied since the last general officer command had moved out of the Munich area. When Dr. Klitzke departed, the Army offered to move us into his house in Gruenwald, but we declined because we felt our children had settled well into the military community at Perlacher and didn't need further dislocation.

But then the Army, having somehow determined that we were truly from the same planet, offered us the "General's House"! After some hemming and hawing, including the condition that we would not be asked to move again during our tour, we agreed to move in.

It was a fine set of quarters: an extra bedroom, a sun porch, a non-G.I. winter-garden room, white carpeting and upgraded furnishings, a grand piano in the living room, and other perks inside and out made it a nice place to live and entertain in.

But what to our wondering eyes should appear, just one year later, but a real general. With becoming embarrassment the Army tried to interest him in alternative housing, but nothing would do for him but the house we were living in. The Army was caught in a bind; not only did we have a gentlemen's agreement about not moving, but I could have gotten into an "equivalent rank" dispute, and probably won the right to stay in the house.

But I feared it would be a Pyrrhic victory. I still had to work with them for CGG's housing, transportation, and all other support matters, and to live in their community, along with my people. I chose to go, as graciously as possible.

The Army upgraded and redecorated a colonel's house in Perlacher (next door to where we were living) and assigned it general's perks, etc., and away we went once again.

The short term disadvantage was the Army's, because the general in question turned out to be a real loser, and ended up being cashiered out of the Army (and thrown out of his quarters in Munich!) because of sordid misadventures with his secretary and the Army's money.

A longer term disadvantage was to son John, who developed a lasting distaste for the Army as a result of the exercise. It came at a time when he was considering a possible appointment to West Point, and he declined out of hand to pursue it. Given the Vietnam situation, it may well have been for the best.

But the long term advantage seems to have been to CGG. When I returned to visit Munich a year or so after leaving, I found three (going on four!)of the twelve houses on Perlacher's colonel's row were occupied by CGG seniors—as compared to a total of none some four or five years earlier. Perhaps a coincidence, perhaps not . . .

GERMANY II – THE MUNICH EXPERIENCE (THE JOB)

In between the attention given to all the support requirements and potential change of job activities covered in previous chapters, I really did find time to go to work in Munich.

The office was housed in a building requisitioned by the U.S. under the occupation agreements; it was actually an ivy-covered private mansion located in one of Munich's high-rent residential suburbs. Formerly the residence of some SS general officer, it was really a nifty place for our purposes.

Madison Mitchell and I had discovered it in late '62, during our numerous trips from Frankfurt. With the help of some U.S. Navy occupants, we enjoyed securing it for our new mission. It was Mitch's passionate wish to avoid having the local CIA office serve as our landlords—an arrangement which would have eased the Army's local logistic problems, but would have destroyed our comfort level. In a slight misuse of the phrase, Mitch's pride of place turned out to have been correct.

I had been especially pleased at the support the U.S. Army furnished us during those early days, even before we moved the office to Munich. Later, I was extra-specially pleased at being able to return funds to the Agency as a result of the "free" services we wangled from the Army, as they helped us out with the necessary investments required for CGG's new home.

The people who staffed CGG were first class. As noted, the Group consisted of a mix of U.S. and U.K. types, with an integrated detachment of service folks from the U.S. Air Force. All of the staff had been pre-selected, and all were more than up to their job requirements. Most of them were professionals, with area and language specialties, but the "non" professionals—who made the place run—were at least equally top notch.

What they all did was interesting and important, but will not be a subject for this paper. You can trust me when I say they all earned their keep!

In '67 the Chief CGG was a true gentleman by the name of Carl F. Klitzke, then in the final year of his tour. He was the second Chief in CGG's brief history—replacing Madison Mitchell who had run early operations in Frankfurt and had moved with the group to Munich.

Dr. Klitzke had been my first "big" boss when I reported to work at Arlington Hall in Jan-Feb 1952. His wife-to-be, Ellie Carman, was my first supervisor then. In '64 Dr. K. became my boss again, when I was chief of staff in B Group where he was deputy chief to Frank Austin.

And now once more I worked for him, this time as deputy and heir-apparent. He was a quiet man, very soft-spoken and unassertive, but well experienced in the business from the wartime days at Arlington Hall. By the Munich years he was approaching the end of his career. More than willing to pass on the reins, he allowed me to assume responsibility for most operational matters; yet his continued presence as chief was unquestioned, and remained most important to the mission.

In two ways, really. His well established reputation, his "Dr." title, and his scholarly demeanor both in the office and among his peers provided the stability which made it possible for this new group to survive its early days. (Dr. K.'s composure also sanctioned the onset of changes which were about to occur—which is to say that his calm made the waves I was causing more navigable.)

In the second place, he and Ellie were superb hosts for the many business and social functions which were critical to the Group's representational responsibilities. While the Klitzkes were a tough act to follow in this respect, they were excellent models for Betty and me to emulate.

The CGG experiment had by then four years on the books. It had grown to be a useful part of the scene, and showed promise of becoming even more so. But as a new broom, I felt compelled to work at hurrying up the process of change. Not <u>always</u> a good idea, and <u>almost never</u> without some pain.

One of the first things we tried was to update the physical work flow. That involved changing the locations of the operations work center, which was met by something short of total enthusiasm on the part of the operations group.

Nevertheless, shortly after my re-arrival at CGG we found it necessary to do additional rehab. I must tell one tale from that experience—one which, among several others, made me question the validity of the Germans' reputation for efficiency.

One consequence of the move required digging out part of the basement, installing some plumbing, and replacing the concrete flooring we had had to remove to do the work. The Army took on the job, contracting it out to local construction firms.

The German contractors had two trucks at the site. One of them was to haul away the debris from the digging—mostly, a large amount of first class gravel. The other was to haul in the necessary equipment and materials for recementing the basement. Fair enough so far.

But I began to question "efficiency" 'when I saw two crews, each with its own shovels and wheelbarrows, passing each other with great dexterity on a temporary planked runway into the basement: one of them was hauling the "old" gravel out, and loading it onto truck "A" for disposal; the other was bringing in fresh "new" gravel provided by truck "B", to use in making concrete for repairing the floor!

No matter . . . in the end we had what we wanted. Or at least what I wanted.

CGG's appearance had not been met with unalloyed joy by in-theater intelligence authorities. Understandably so, since part of our reason for being was to augment and improve various existing services. Those who, as far as they were concerned, had been getting along just fine <u>without</u> us were unprepared to let us take over.

It was a bit dicey in the early days: while we didn't intend to (nor could we) "take over" anybody's job but our own, there were some turf battles that had to be fought before there was <u>local</u> acceptance of things which had been worked out in the macrocosms of Washington. In our previous tour in Frankfurt I had had this problem on my plate; as part of that I had been sent back to Washington to help work out what was to become CGG.

Back there we had achieved agreement for NSA (and CGG) to have a policy role in managing some intelligence operations which had become pretty freewheeling over the years. Putting that agreement into practice was our toughest job. No matter . . . that just added spice to the cake.

In due course we got our seats at the various tables involved. Most of the resulting augmentations and improvements were gradually accepted, by some more fully than by others, but in the long run it became a generally worthwhile enterprise. On a personal note, participating in those early days of the CGG experience helped me (indeed, <u>made</u> me) develop a faculty for liaison and interaction which was to become useful in later exercises within the intelligence world.

As noted, Dr. Klitzke's presence did much to help in this phase of the business. Before he left he also supported our early efforts to intensify our technical impact in the Liaison arena. This, too, helped bring far-reaching benefits in later years.

After I became chief, I felt the need to strengthen our ties with the military. The reasons for this urge on my part are probably too complex to describe here—and to do an adequate job of it I would likely slip into classified areas. But in any case the outcome turned out over time to be useful for most of us involved.

The project called for a lot of travel (both on my part and by key staff as well) to various Allied Command Europe sites. We participated in conferences, meetings, briefings, and the whole gamut of learning-who-you-are-and-telling-who-we-are sort of thing. Of course the visits then called for return visits, and more conferences, meetings and briefings.

An invaluable colleague, German Air Force General Staff Colonel Douglas Pitcairn, helped greatly in smoothing entry into some important Bundeswehr activities. Col. Pitcairn had had an illustrious career with the Luftwaffe: learned to fly in the 30's in Hungary, flew with the government forces during the Spanish Revolution, was key to the German defenses at Ploesti, and was shot down into British captivity late in the war. His indefatigable energy and good humor, along with his deeply pro-Western (and in our case pro-American) loyalties made him invaluable to the course of post-war cooperation. After his retirement, and mine, we have enjoyed each other's friendship.

In the course of all this I began to be convinced that our SHAPE common military interests and missions were such an important part of our NATO political involvement that they called for improved service-to-service relationships across international lines. That in itself would make an interesting story—again, I'm afraid, not for this memoir.

At any rate, the work begun in those days, with my CGG hat on continued for the rest of my tour in Munich and well beyond the rest of my years with NSA. From those early insights, I have grown into an advocate of the need for the U.S. to continue to interact militarily with our Western European allies.

[It is not so much my belief that we need to do so for a mutual military defense against a traditional military foe—that danger has receded from prime importance—but it is essentially because we need to play a key role in the international arena for other, more enduring reasons.

Our position as the principal military power in the world makes us indispensable to any workable Western common defense-economic-political system. It is the most lasting key we have to assure entry to that table. To use that key we need to be, and be seen to be, the leading member of the international defense team.]

While the office continued to take more than its share of my time, our tour in Munich had its family allotment as well. The children picked these years to experience their teens, and as Betty and I had been pre-selected to experience them with them, we all had a fairly heavy schedule of experiences!

John and Pi were both teenagers throughout the Munich years; Kathy gained that status a year after we got there (and two years before we left). I can't describe what they went through from the inside—their memoirs, which I would love to read, will have to do that—but it sure looked interesting from the outside!

It was a singular experience for them, and for their parents. They learned how it was to be in a foreign land. And although they lived in an American cocoon, they managed to get out of it from time to see strange folks and strange lands.

We did some traveling together (minus John, who had already outgrown that sort of thing) and they (especially John) did some on their own with comrades. And they enjoyed meeting the many visitors who made their way through our homes, just as we enjoyed showing the children off.

It wasn't all fun and games for them. There were temptations and heartaches and euphoria and despair mixed in—part of the price all of us pay to grow up, but especially tough, even if rewarding—for them. Their mother bore, as usual, the burden of helping them through the maze, while I was, as usual, mostly a self-important Elsewhere, if anything adding unwanted pressure on them by virtue of my job.

Nonetheless, they did a great job of growing up straight and honest and likeable. Not that it is ever easy for teenagers, but it was especially hard in a military environment where drugs and alcohol were everywhere, and the pressures from their peers and the young soldiers to taste those "pleasures" were enormous.

During the second summer we were joined by Betty's folks, Mother and Mac MacDonald. We had a great time with them, and they with us. Their first overseas trip became something special for them; they enjoyed its memories for the rest of their lives.

One of them involved their first night in Germany. Betty and I had met them in Frankfurt, and were planning an auto trip with them down the Rhine, across Germany, and into Scandinavia before returning to Munich. The first stop was to be in Bonn, where I was to have lunch with the U.S. Ambassador.

It was not to be. That night the phone called me into the office as the Russian invasion of Czechoslovakia got under way. Betty's folks had to watch at first hand how the demands of the family were mostly subordinated to the job. It was not until a month or so later that we rescheduled a makeup trip through Belgium, Holland and France, this time without danger of foreign military engagements.

Betty's part of the Munich experience was inestimably important. Not only did she guide the family to safe haven during these years, but she took on the job of being CGG's Senior Lady as if she had been born to it.

She served as the leader of the Office Social Group, entertaining the office wives, listening to the tales of woe the wives had with their overseas situations, helping them to understand and cope with the intrusions made into their lives by our military hosts and by their CGG workplace.

Additionally, Betty had to see that the various official parties and semi-official entertainments we were called on to give and/or to attend could take place at minimum disruption to our family life. She was always more than up to the job. Her abilities to handle demanding social occasions with grace and good humor won us all many friends. In fact, once she insisted that a visiting Director be pressed—against his will—to attend a reception just for our office family, and was able to make him enjoy it.

On this same visit—one of the last and most senior of the parties to visit during our tour—Betty contributed significantly to my later assignment on the Director's staff. The Director, Adm. Gayler, Gen. Morrison, Gen. Fenili, Mitt Matthews, and several others descended on us.

Interspersed with the briefings and visits which the CGG staff (especially the invaluable Dick Vayhinger) arranged, there were visits to the Opera (two), an official office party, a brunch prepared at home by Betty (on Mother's Day, no less!), and a couple visits to some high-class lowbrow Bier halls. Her help in guiding us through all that made a great impression on our visitors.

And finally, Betty's insistence on going to "stand on at least one Alp" before we left Germany led to my re-learning how to handle myself on skis, and ultimately enabled me to ski the slopes of the Zugspitze with the admiral, thus gaining a valuable plus on my report card.

Betty also had to (and did!) help me through two very tearing personal losses, as both my brother Bill and my mother died while we were on this tour. In both cases the deaths were unexpected, especially Bill's (who died on the Happy Valley golf course, at age 54). I returned home to Lynn in the summer of '68 for my brother's funeral, only to return once more in December to help bury my mother.

Almost before I could be aware of it, our tour and my two years as chief were ending. The final act was to be the traditional farewell visits to the partners in our common enterprises. There were many, but I will cite only two.

First there was a formal farewell celebration with some German Army friends at their base in the Eifel. The German commander (Col. Eichhorn) was a wartime veteran, like me, and even more mindful that, not too many years before, his command area had been the location of the frozen horror we recall as the Bulge.

I will not forget the poignancy of the pre-war military honors ceremony of that evening, with the officers and their ladies in full dress and the haunting tones of the Waldhorns sounding as if from afar . . . . In retrospect (and possibly at the time as well, though I honestly cannot recall) it was a healing experience for both Eichhorn and myself; it marked for us an ending and a beginning in a way which cannot be described, but which we both understood.

The second was during the visit to the German navy base at Flensburg. What I remember from there was not so much the official ceremony, but a far less formal goodbye luncheon at the commander's home. There, after a straightforward seaman's lunch, Captain Winter and I sealed another farewell with a warm handshake.

Why this is so memorable is that this was the same Winter who commanded the U-Boat which shadowed our WWII convoy across the Atlantic on our way to France. Elsewhere I have written about how our ship escaped without harm. But Captain Winter and I shared a special thankfulness that our stars had permitted another ending and beginning.

Selecting but two of the farewells means by <u>no</u> means that the rest are not gratefully treasured. Those by the Luftwaffe and the MOD and the special set of goodbye's arranged by "the Pullachers" all have their distinct places in warm memory—as do the many valedictories by our CGG family which, more than any of the others, helped ease the stresses and strains of our return home.

(I don't recall any huge commemorative celebrations on the part of the official Munich military community, but several private occasions by some of its members are still gratefully remembered.)

And thus it was back to Fort Meade, and the final chapters of our working lives at NSA. But I can't finish the story of our Munich tour without recalling the words of Dr. Tordella to me as I was leaving the building in 1967 on our way to Munich: "You'll find, Harney, that the worst thing about your new job is that you'll never be able to have it again." How right he was.

RETURN TO FORT MEADE

With the dust of our last overseas tour swirling around us, we departed Munich for our return to New Carrollton and Fort Meade. Not that we left without incident, beginning with our final goodbyes to the CGG family at the airport; they had all gathered at the Munchen Riem Airport to wave us away, the kind of personal farewell that was still possible in those days before obsession with security had taken over all comings and goings at airports.

So, after the last sip of champagne the flight was called, and we left waving and waving, only to find out after the first fifty yards of our journey that our flight was messed up, and we would have to wait for the next one. Hiding ourselves behind some magazine racks, we avoided having to return to our waved-out CGGers and their empty champagne bottles.

We did get to Frankfurt on the next flight, and arranged to spend the night at the Ambassador Arms, where my passport wallet and various ID's disappeared, never to be recovered. The reconstruction of my official identity took much time and all the patience everyone involved could muster. No matter, we arrived back in the States without further incident.

Once again we avoided the opportunity to move from New Carrollton to some new, more promising address. And once again it was a combination of reluctance on the part of the children and inertia on my own part. As always I was self-directed to the challenges of the new job, and some of the really more important things took a back seat.

To cover them adequately would require a much deeper look at myself and all of us than I am prepared to undertake at the moment although I will return to the subject in other chapters if the Good Lord is willing and the keyboard holds up!

Let me say only, before resuming with the final years of my career with NSA, that the family had a bit more difficulty in adjusting to this stage of our lives than we had had before. Perhaps it was a natural consequence of reaching "transitions", each coming to bridges of various kinds at about the same time, perhaps not. But at any rate, I can look back at those years and say, at the very worst, that we weathered them and reached safe harbors, together.

I reported to my new job as Deputy Chief of the Foreign Relations Division. My boss was Larry Terry, whom I had three years earlier barely avoided replacing in Frankfurt. I was not to remain in this assignment for more than a few months, but it was not without its value.

I was eager to widen my focus to include areas other than Europe. Once before, in my brief tour as a Group Chief-of-Staff, I had begun to do so, but that experience was cut short by the assignment to the War College. Now I would be able to try it again.

The foreign relations business, with its tricky ties with the CIA and elsewhere, was a particular province of Dr. Tordella. As late as my post-Munich assignment its control was still closely held in his hands. I had grown up under this situation and felt comfortable with it.

With Dr. Tordella's OK, my first order of business was to arrange a tour of key Pacific and Far Eastern outposts. With an old "China" hand, Hank DeCourt, I set out for Japan in what must have been one of R&D models of the Boeing 747, creaking, sighing, even leaking(condensation, I was almost sure!). We plowed westward on the longest jet flight I had had up until then.

Without dwelling overlong on this particular tile in the mosaic, I cannot overemphasize the import of this trip for future assignments. While the first visit to the Far East is generally described in terms of hot tub baths at the Sanno and Ke Song(?) parties in Seoul, a locker room like practice, it was so much more.

Coming face to face with Asians and their approach to the security business, seeing our own Pacific Commands at first hand in the vastness of their defense tasks, and sensing the changes that we would have to come to grips with in the Pacific Rim of the future, even as we were concentrating on the mire that was Vietnam, were all eye-openers to me. As usual, I was left with the understanding that I had much to learn before I would be of any value in this new venue about to be added to the old.

We covered many miles in three weeks or so: Tokyo and Japan (with Bob Rich as the local honcho); Seoul and Korea (with Jim Harris); Okinawa (with John Eastman and Fred Cole?); Taipei and Taiwan (with Bob Painter), and home again via Honolulu's various headquarters (with Dave Boak).

One of the lasting non-business memories is of marveling at the panoply of fall-colored trees that passed below our small plane as we moved north toward Hokkaido. Their awesome splendor brought back the memory of the blaze of colors in the New England autumns of my youth, and reminded me also of similar overwhelming days in Germany, in the fall of 1945 when I was still in the Army. All this together, tumbling in the mind of one far from home and family, made me once again aware our world, despite the enormity of its geography, is a pretty small place.

I was immediately beset by a scheme for two business ventures, either of which could have made me a wealthy man, but neither of which I followed up. The first was the thought of arranging for off-season golf and hotels in Myrtle Beach, which in the 70's was growing faster than its customer base, and leasing some 747 flights from Tokyo to ferry Japanese golfers to the courses. What would have frosted the cake was the idea of recruiting some of our retired Phoenician Japanese linguists to serve as tour guides and hand-holders. (Of course I didn't do it, and some years later ferrying Japanese golfers became a huge money-maker in the Pacific.)

The second brainstorm was to export some of the early virtual golf systems (where you used your own clubs to hit a ball around a virtual-video course) to Japan. Remember, in those days the U.S. was still in the lead in this sort of thing, but no matter, still no action.

The trip ended in early November, I believe, and I settled back into the new job with interest. That lasted for about a month, when I was tabbed for another job, this one as Executive Assistant to the Director. This move was to put me into the top levels of NSA management, and though I was not yet to be one of the top level managers, it was to lead sooner rather than later to that outcome.

Executive Assistantry will follow . . . .

EXECUTIVE ASSISTANT TO THE DIRECTOR TOUR

The executive assistant job was established by General Carter. I understood he intended it to be similar to the executive officer posts in the Army, modified somewhat by the executive assistants he had seen in the CIA at the directorate level. Carter selected Jerry Burke as his EAD, and Jerry's intelligence, ability and personality led them to build the job into a combination Chief of Staff/Exec/Factotum.

Owing in large part to General Carter's own personality and personal agenda—which made him a very likeable man but undermined his ability to function as well as some of us had hoped and expected—a cleft developed between the Director and his staff and the rest of the agency. Too bad, for he was a man of unusual abilities, assisted by another man of great talent, Jerry Burke. But to follow their act, I believed, would be unwise. So I chose not to do so.

Admiral Noel Gayler, then Director of NSA, selected me as his EAD from a batch of nominees. I believe it was largely due to his TDY trip to Germany in the late spring of 1970. At that time he visited CGG and, with great assists from our competent staff there, he must have left with some pretty positive views of CGG and its chief.

(This visit is covered in more, although far from complete, detail in the Munich Part II section of this book. I don't believe I mentioned there anything about my day with Admiral Gayler on the slopes of Zugspitze: the opportunity we had for a heart-to-heart, person-to-person session while leaning on our ski poles, likely provided additional foundation for his choosing me for his Executive Assistant.)

Whatever the reason, I moved into the job, replacing Bob Sears, who had briefly replaced Jerry, in December of 1970. It was my first assignment in the top-most command structure of the Agency and the Cryptologic System. As usual, I came to the job with serious doubts as to my readiness for it. Here was the Director—The Admiral—already a controversial figure as I was to find out—who wanted me to help him run the strange place he had been given to direct.

His first words were that he wanted someone who understood the Agency and its people and their methods, someone in whom he might confide and who would give him straightforward speed and heading warnings when he seemed to need them. At least that's how I interpreted what he said. To the extent that that is what he did say, I fear I did not fully meet the task.

He was not a man who was easily guided, almost never directly by his subordinates, and seldom by his peers. And yet he was a man of great intelligence who could be moved—better, one who could move himself onto the right courses, if only he could be convinced. To use Navy talk, he was not a ship you could readily take under tow, but he knew how to benefit from the occasional nudge from the tugboat.

While I was not able to meet his desired requirements fully, nor was probably anyone else, I could do some other things which I think may have helped him a bit, and some of which I think were of value to the Agency and to him. Oh, I do hope so!

[The major exception was Mitt Matthews, for whom Admiral Gayler had great respect and affection along with enormous professional admiration. Mitt would have been the only one I know who might have answered all the Admiral's wishes. But he was too valuable to move, too senior for the job, and, alas, too mortal. He died on the R&D director job, half way through Admiral Gayler's tour as Director (coincidentally very shortly after my appointment had been announced); his loss to us all was enormous.]

I began to see early on that one part of my job might have to be that of a bridge builder. Admiral Gayler's personality did not allow him to suffer fools gladly. Unfortunately, it also caused him to make the "fool" judgment too quickly, often rashly, and sometimes for the wrong reasons. It led to a situation where he was cutting himself off from some of the Agency's best people, juniors whose knowledge and technical abilities he needed to do his job successfully, and seniors whose support and loyalty were key to the process. It was my job to keep him from hurting himself.

I did share my feelings with him on this point, and he did take them aboard. But I believe the problem, though it might have been alleviated somewhat, did not go away. You know the old saying, "What's bred in the bone, etc." Junior analysts and specialists of all kinds were often frightened by him, and some avoided the occasions of his presence.

But the Agency needed to understand him better as well. One had to expect a certain amount of impatience with the ways of bureaucracy, even a good one like ours, from a man whose earlier commands had included major combat vessels. When you command an aircraft carrier you are accustomed to standing on the bridge in complete charge, and when you say "Launch all aircraft" there is a certain amount of immediate response to your command, like, all hell breaks loose and the planes take off!

When, as Director of NSA, you stand at your desk and say "Fix all those field directives!", the only immediate response is the echoing of your own voice down the long hallways. The first tangible reaction you are apt to get is some weeks later when an irate, very senior field commander may call you and ask, "What in hell are you doing to my SIGINT?!!" This difference in the time and nature of responses to one's directions tends to breed or to feed impatience. And we did not always allow for that when we judged him.

One continuing task I had was to keep track of the "commands" the Admiral issued. The number of actions his prolific intelligence generated was staggering. The scope of his interests knew few bounds. I filled notebook after notebook with action items, and had to devise systems to keep track of them all. It became clear that neither the Agency's people nor the Admiral would have had time to respond adequately if all the items were to be fully actioned. It became a matter of determining priorities, hoping to guess which would survive the changing attentions of the Director, and holding one's breath at staff meeting time!

My time as Admiral Gayler's EAD was exciting, exhilarating, and exhausting. It took all of my attention and most of my energy just to cope. But it was hugely instructive in all its parts. It opened up the top-most levels of the cryptologic community to me, and me to them. Despite my nagging self-doubts at the time, I am, in retrospect, less harsh on my performance as a would-be executive, the Admiral never faulted me, after all, and more confident that my efforts at bridge building were useful to the Agency and the community both. (Though time and circumstance have separated us from continuing personal contact, I continue to view Admiral Gayler with warm personal regard and unswerving professional respect. I believe him to have been one of the Agency's better directors, in a time which was truly a watershed in our history.)

The hallmark, or one of the hallmarks of Admiral Gayler's directorship was the imposition of the CSS, the Central Security Service, onto the cryptologic system. "Imposition" is an accurate descriptor, since the CSS really arose out of our efforts to comply with a special presidential directive. The directive was a well-intended attempt to help solidify NSA controls over the Service cryptologic agencies. Unfortunately, it was wide of the mark. (I sense that a word of explanation may be in order here. I will try to be brief, but this whole area embraced such a large part of my career duties that it requires some understanding if I am to be understood).

NSA was established by the President in the early 1950's and "put in charge" of all U.S. SIGINT operations. The chartering directive gave NSA operational and technical control over all such operations no matter who carried them out. It was clear and concise. So much so that almost everyone involved began to argue its "real" meaning almost before the ink had dried.

It's not appropriate to discuss the details of the arguments here, but it will be helpful to understand the CSS part of the story to know that one of the principal areas of disagreement centered on the degree to which NSA's controls embraced "tactical" SIGINT. Tactical means that which is needed to allow the armed services principally, but other executive agencies as well, to carry out the "tactical" activities. There was a lot of to and fro over definitions, some of which I am sure is still going on today.

By Admiral Gayler's tour, there had been such dispute over words that some interested parties in the White House decided to put an end to it by giving the Director, NSA, literal "Command" authority over all those who were involved in doing SIGINT. That included elements of the Army, Navy, Air Force, Marine Corps, and CIA, to name only the bigger ones. Oops! Now you've got it, NSA. Let's hear no more bickering. The only problem was that it would have been impossible for any executive agency, especially a largely civilian one like NSA, to exercise "command" over parts of the Army, Navy, etc.

To make the story shorter, NSA had to find a way to answer the directive, to satisfy those in the White House who were trying to help, without terminally offending those whose SIGINT operations it was already charged to control operationally and technically.

Our putative answer became the Central Security Service. Briefly once more, the CSS was ostensibly to be an organization of those elements outside NSA, primarily military, which did SIGINT, when they did SIGINT. It approached the "command" problem by putting its command structure under a military officer (two star) who reported to the Director, NSA, but was not to be otherwise subject to NSA's civilian control. The idea was imaginative, but turned out to be far from workable.

Back to my Executive Assistant role in all this. I became the Director's surrogate in the drafting of the CSS charter. It involved forming and participating in the dozen or so steering committees which finessed an impossible organizational problem by turning toward functional area issues instead. The product was a fairly responsive, quite detailed report to the Secretary of Defense, out of which came the organization of the CSS. I will not comment further, except to say that the work we all did apparently satisfied our real purposes, namely to stay alive to fight another day. I will return later to the issues of operational and technical control which were so central to my career at NSA.

Fortunately the more important work of the Agency and the system continued while this was going on. The war in Southeast Asia had about reached its maximum levels and required extraordinary attention. While the Cold War continued to occupy its portion of center stage as well. Rapid advances in technology offered great new challenges both to keep pace with changes in target activities and in evolving new ways to improve our own. The Director and his staff were well occupied in seeking effective ways to manage attendant growth and change. It was an exciting, exhausting time.

I was in the EAD job for just about a year and a half. Even today I cannot believe that was all it lasted. But when it was over, the Admiral moved on to become CINCPAC, the Commander-in-Chief of U.S. forces in the Pacific. Before he left he saw to a new job for me as CINC-Schools (I jest), the Commandant of the National Cryptologic School and the Director of Training for the Central Security Service. At the outset of this new assignment I was afraid that the size of the title, it took a double door to accommodate it, would be the biggest part of the job. But more about that in the next chapter.

THE COMMANDANT YEAR

My time as the Executive Assistant ended when Admiral Gayler left NSA to become the Commander-in-Chief of U.S. forces in the Pacific. It was an enormous step up for him. Admiral Gayler won his fourth star, the first NSA director to become a four-star officer, and moved into the CINCPAC job as the war in Vietnam approached its final stages.

I should not let him move out of my active life without saying once more how much I liked and admired him, not only as a Chief, but also as a person. His WWII heroics distinguished him as one of the outstanding warriors of the U.S. Navy in the Pacific. In the process he also acquired a perspective on war and its lethal costs which is granted only to those who have personally seen them being exacted. He developed private anti-nuclear warfare views, crystallized no doubt by his intimate association with nuclear warfare planning at JSTPC. In time he made these views public, which did not make him the Navy's favorite flag officer.

As the Admiral was leaving NSA he awarded me the post of Commandant of the National Cryptologic School. The job, fortuitously, became open when Frank Austin, a sterling Commandant, decided to retire. I am confident the Director wanted to look out for me by giving me this assignment, but it would not have been my first choice. While the School was an important part of the system, it was by no means in the front line. The Commandant's job had mostly been occupied by distinguished NSA veterans, chief among them its first, the illustrious Frank Rowlett, at the twilight of their careers. It was not known for being a platform from which to move onward.

Like a good soldier, I accepted the responsibility for the School with only mild reservation, made milder by the challenge of making the training system for the CSS a working reality. This came from one of the features of the newly created CSS: the functional consolidation of the various Service cryptologic schools and NSA's National Cryptologic School. It had been named the Training System of the CSS, but not yet fully defined. As Commandant, I was to be its Director.

Frank Austin had done a fine job of working out the outlines of the CSS Training System, and his vision became the roadmap we included in the CSS report to the Secretary of Defense. Now it was up to me to get it done. Accordingly, as I moved to my new desk, I set as my first years priority the actions required to understand the Services' individual training programs, and to work out with them a meaningful, productive, and acceptable consolidation. Not a centralization, a consolidation!

Despite the added challenge, moving from my ninth floor perch in the middle of the battle, to the calm backwaters of the school was a personal wrench, to put it mildly. I left a world where the eight hour day was unheard of (the sixty-four hour week was more like it), to one where it was the upper side of the norm. It took me a while to adjust.

At any rate, I moved into place as gracefully as I could, and began to learn about the training system, beginning with the National Cryptologic School. It turned out to be quite a place. Instruction was in good shape, with excellent people writing courses and teaching them. Administration of the various faculties seemed in capable hands, and the support staff (Registrar, Audio-Visual, programs and budget, and operations) were very good to excellent. They seemed healthy enough to withstand the incursions of a neophyte commandant. So, with very few exceptions, I decided to let them go their own way for that first year, and I would turn a more experienced attention to them in the second year which, ironically, I was not going to have as their Commandant.

I was fortunate to have some good folks on board. Chief among these was probably George McGuiness, my Navy Captain Deputy. George is one of the real old Navy hands, with enough cryptologic experience and enough respect for both the Navy and NSA to be helpful in a time when understanding between military and civilian components of the system was important. The Navy cryptologic service was the senior service in the NSA-CSS. During my career it had always been a special problem for NSA in our efforts to exercise the presidentially mandated op— and techcon over the services. It had to do with the requirements and privileges the Navy has claimed and won based on the special nature of command at sea. George was very helpful in interpreting this for us, and in helping us to win the Navy's support where it was to be won.

As I have written, the faculty and administrative staff had some very good folks as well. They were patient with the interloper, with me, and kept the school doing its job while I was busy elsewhere. I made the rounds of the Service cryptologic schools: Army at Fort Devens, Navy at Pensacola, Air Force at Goodfellow, and even the Defense Language School, in which we had critical interests, at Monterey. I also checked in on key overseas field stations where major OJT operations were being carried out. I felt, and still believe, that we needed a good understanding of what the Services were doing before we attempted to put any handles on them. And I used the process to do a little propagandizing of my own views that this process of consolidation or coordination, or streamlining, whatever, was to be a jointly arrived at, agreed arrangement to the extent possible. There was a hammer in there somewhere, but I wanted all to understand that we should not put ourselves in a position where it had to be used. I left the job unfinished, but I am confident that it had been moved forward along the lines that our plan had called for, and that Frank Austin had begun.

By the time I had gotten to this point, the bell rang again, and I had been ordered to a new job in the Pentagon. I never did get to the next objective, where I would have had a good enough grasp on the curricula or the faculty to make any impact at all on the school's basic mission. Apart from making some speeches and posing for some pictures, and leading some foreign visitors around the premises, my contributions in that area were negligible. While I did take some steps to shore up the ties between the operations areas, for whom we really existed, and the school, that was more a statement of philosophy than a course of action.

I left the Commandant's desk with the feeling I had never earned the right to the impressive titles the position carried. On the other hand, in my subsequent visits to the school and its people, both before and after retirement, I had the feeling that they were doing just fine. I guess at least I did no harm.

THE PENTAGON (PART II)

After I had barely begun to get my feet wet at the National Cryptologic School, the call came for me to get ready to return to the Pentagon—after six years—to replace Herb Conley as the Senior NSA Representative in (not "to", mind you) the Pentagon. During my first tour in the Pentagon I had found fault with the nature of NSA's presence there, and had recommended to one of our internal review panels that we should upgrade our office there in a number of ways. It was important to us, I believed, both for style and substance. One of the features of the New NSA Pentagon representative was to be a senior cryptologist chief, of comparable grade to the flag/general officers and upper-level DOD civilians we had to make mudpies with in order for NSA to do its job adequately.

The recommendation was adopted and a senior NSA'er was appointed the first chief under the new rules (1970?-71?). In due course, I became the fourth NSA Senior rep in June of 1973. It was kind of "law of unintended consequences", since I believed I had served my penance out in the first Pentagon assignment, but there was no escaping it. The sweetener was that I had become a GS-18 and would fit the new requirements (which I had suggested as a substantive component for the job to have its needed panache). So, it was goodbye Commandant, Hello NSA Rep Defense and welcome to the top levels of Agency managers, after 21 ½ years in the business.

In a way it was a return to the frying pan. An early morning commute, a late evening drive home—fortunately by this time I had Flag Officer reserved parking, but it all led to the same old building—and in between a daily regimen in which crisis was often routine.

This tour was a bit different personally from the first one: the carry-over from our return from Munich had been harder on the family in many ways than the return from Frankfurt. The children were deep into their teens—John had graduated high school in Munich and was deciding where and whether to go to college, Mary Ellen and Kathy's expectations had both been seriously affected by court-ordered integration in Prince Georges County, and their final years in high school were not happy ones for them. Perhaps most significantly, the rigorous work and social involvements of the last years had taken a heavy toll on Betty and me.

It was a very wearing experience. For the very first time, I found it difficult to concentrate on my job, a tough hurdle in this new milieu. By good chance, I had a very competent staff to help me at the office, and the family got the rest straightened out before lasting harm could settle in.

The previous tenants had spent much of their time assiduously establishing the office and themselves with the civilian-military hierarchy of the Defense Department. With more than a little success, not surprising considering their talents and backgrounds. I benefitted from the ties they had strengthened, and the new ones they had established. Plus, the independent office and increase in rank made access to the real powers freer; the perks of rank (choice of parking, membership in the SecDef mess, etc) made it all more livable.

But as working the SecDef bureaucracy was not really my thing, I chose to operate more closely with the Armed Services and the Joint Staff on a number of other issues that had interested me and had been of concern to NSA over the years. That is, I chose when I had the choice; meaning only in those periods when I was not driven by circumstance, crisis, or specific tasks assigned me by the Agency—which was much of the time.

We were still in the early days of the Central Security Service. The Armed Services had been spooked by the language of the presidential directive—calling for NSA to take "command" of the service cryptologic agencies. NSA's best efforts to create a non-threatening CSS did not dispel the clouds. Persisting Service fears that a centralized, "national-oriented", civilian influenced organization would fail to give sufficient attention to military needs threatened serious dissolution in the SIGINT System: one we had spent the last two-plus decades constructing. First to go was the Army (ASA), followed by the Air Force (AFSS). The Navy (NSG) was not specifically detached, but that made little difference. (That's a bit unfair: the Navy had made significant contributions to the national cryptologic mission, and acted its part in the system when it did not conflict with the overriding Navy matters. But there was always that card to play, even though it was not called for very often).

The Army was engaged in one of their recurring umbilico-skeptical operations, this one called the IOSS—"Intelligence Organization and Staffing Study". It had major implications for the Army Security Agency, the army's component in the CSS and more importantly, the U.S. SIGINT System. The general in charge used to consult frequently with our office, specifically me, in an honest effort to learn what implications a proposed Army disengagement might bring with it. He was a bright young major general—his name is gone from me in this senior moment—who seemed willing to negotiate.

I had been from the early days an advocate for the US SIGINT system, composed of an NSA primusinterpares and its important service (and other) components.* Accordingly I worked very hard to convince the Army study group that our System could indeed accommodate Army requirements, and that in fact we could do a better job if the Army component remained within it.

It probably made little difference I expect, since the Army seemed to have had its head made up. The result of the IOSS review was the incorporation of what was ASA into an Army Intelligence Command (INSCOM), and in my view a serious weakening of the Army's ability to contribute. I was unable to convince our Director, Gen. Lew Allen— the best we ever had, by the way—to intervene; he was never one to be terribly concerned about organization, and he may well have been right not to expend his time and talents on this target. Lord knows he spent them most fruitfully on many other arguably more important tasks.

The Air Force component, the AFSS, was soon to follow. Valid Air Force concerns about integration of intelligence and operations, especially in electronic warfare countermeasures, formed the basis for a similar action on their part. Once again the SIGINT System was weakened—in my view—by the effective withdrawal of one of its major components. I was not directly involved in Air Force deliberations in the Pentagon or elsewhere. Come to think of it, I'm not even certain when they happened, but my imperfect memory would have me believe they followed the Army move.

The impressive ECM programs the Air Force has been able to bring to pass may or may not have been achievable under the AFSS/SIGINT System arrangement. In any case I was not substantively involved.

This change in the system mix was exaggerated by a trend toward recentralization of operations at NSA. Forced in large part by budgetary pressures, overseas activities were severely cut back. Advances in technology enabled reorientation of operations which had traditionally been carried out for the system by the service cryptologic agencies. In retrospect, those of us who were arguing for a continuation of the past were, as is inevitably the case, overwhelmed by the present. Since I left before the future had fully arrived, I cannot comment further.

The second major development of this second Pentagon tour centered on NSA's efforts to improve support to military operations. We had already seen excellent results from the Cryptologic Support Group program, by which experienced NSA analysts were integrated at major U.S. military commands at home and abroad. We were in the process of expanding the program and improving it, we thought, by bringing our integrated analysts closer to the operations staffs at the supported military commands. Silly us! Once again we had stepped into someone's rice bowl. So our Pentagon staff was called upon to help clean it up.

The crux of the matter was about whether bringing our product and system capabilities closer to the operator (the J3-G3-S3's) would interfere with the responsibilities of the various service intelligence staffs (the J2-G2-S2's). This issue had been smoldering since my early days with the Agency, but this was one of the occasions when it threatened to burst into flame. General Allen had created a special group (headed by Bob Hermann) to find ways to improve support to tactical military operations. This was one of their key recommendations.

My job was to help the agency, Bob Hermann in particular, explain to the Services why this was a good idea, Unfortunately, we adopted the rational course of going to the operators—since they were the ones we felt had the major stake in being supported—and substantiating why our proposal was in their interests. The results were twofold: one, the service operators thought it was not a bad idea—once we had had a chance privately to interpret Bob's sometimes esoteric language; second, the service intelligence guys thought it was <u>not</u> a good idea, and were, in part, incensed that we had gone to talk to the operational folks directly. (Incidentally, the part that was incensed was the ONI, whose director was Bobby Inman).

Despite this early flak, I believe the principle involved has developed into acceptable, and I believe useful, variations. I certainly hope so.

The rest of the Pentagon tour wound itself down. I was occupied seriously with getting senior military commanders to visit NSA and learn what we could—in some cases could not—do for them. Arranging and accompanying various notables on the helicopter hops out to the buildings at Meade was an experience. The cast of characters ranged over some very different types of personality. At the poles were Gen Al Haig, perhaps the most affable, on his way to his job as SACEUR, and Jim Schlesinger, certainly the least, as he worked his way into his activist tour as SecDef. While Haig and I philosophized together about the transitoriness of glory (I did not know then that he was not really committed to the principle), Schlesinger barely accepted that I was alive, preferring to read the comics in that morning's <u>Post.</u> In any case I enjoyed flying almost directly over our modest home in New Carrollton, in the company of some of the movers and shakers of our times.

Despite Schlesinger's demeanor in the chopper, he was really impressed by his day-long visit at NSA. So much so that he "recommended" similar visits to the Joint Chiefs. Barely had I gotten into the office the next day when the phones lit up from the aides of all the senior four stars in the JCS, and several of the senior three-stars. We arranged what had to be the most star-filled visit to Ft Meade in its history to that date.

In due course two choppers filled with these notables arrived at Tipton airfield, I recall vividly even today the profanity laced bewilderment of the air-traffic warrant in charge when the pilots announced the ranks of their incoming passengers. No one (including me) had told them in advance of this truly wondrous visit.

The Chiefs et al were duly briefed and returned to their duties. I don't think they were as impressed as was Gentleman Jim, but their backgrounds and interests were not identical. All in all, however, I believe the program the Agency adopted to brief in some depth senior military officers was valuable. While there was, and is, I suspect, no way to eliminate cultural chasms that exist between the military and non-military, the occasional bridge can help us all better live with the differences.

The remainder of the tour involved much routine, occasionally interrupted by the unusual. Part of the routine involved business lunches and associations, and some social activities—I remember fondly the visit Mother and Grampy MacDonald made to the Pentagon, where I was able to give them some feel for the things I had not been able to tell them about my life. And lunch with Betty and her parents in the Secretary's dining room was certainly a highlight for all of us.

Visits from foreign dignitaries abounded, from the Korean intelligence folks, with whom we tried to establish some level of understandable conversation, to the head of our British counterparts at GCHQ. When I introduced Sir Leonard (Joe) Hooper to Secretary Schlesinger, shirt sleeved at his massive desk, Mr. Schlesinger got us off to a great start when he said, "So, this is one of the guys who is going to tip us off when civilization as we know it is about to end." But we stumbled through.

Then there was a tour of the Atlantic and Pacific theater bases on one of the repeating investigations of airborne collection operations. One or two memories intrude on our factual findings: first, as Admiral Gayler's guests (he was then CINCPAC) we were quartered on Oahu in the sumptuous accommodations the Admiral's father had architected(?). Later, in Rota, Spain, I bought the best putter I ever owned, and left it at the golf course. A bright LtCdr—later to become a very bright admiral—retrieved it and sent it on to me, where in due course it disappeared into the bag of son John. It couldn't have found a better home.

Then, finally, I was recalled to duty at NSA, Ft Meade, where I was to serve out my last five years, as a true NSA senior.

*Ironically, one of the later directors of NSA—Admiral Bobby Inman—came to NSA with a notion that I was among a powerful few NSA senior civilians who were anti-military control over the agency, to the point where they were working to bring about a civilian director. The truth that I was never a member of such a group never fully overcame his suspicions, I fear, and may have colored his views. I retired from the agency prematurely—principally because I was unable to win his full confidence. The irony is that when I left I was still fully committed to maintaining a strong military-civilian partnership.

BACK TO FT. MEADE – THE ASSISTANT DIRECTOR YEARS

With the second installment of my Pentagon penance behind me, it was time to return to Fort Meade and take on the tasks which were to occupy the rest of my years with NSA (Fall '75 to Feb '80).

My immediate replacement in the Pentagon was Jerry Burke—a switch from when I had replaced him as EAD. I went back to a job which had been created especially for me, an Agency directorate charged with management of policy and oversight of a complex of liaison activities. It moved me into the top level of Agency managers as an Assistant Director.

I was as pleased as punch at this assignment. For the first time since I had started to move up the management chain I felt comfortable at my prospects of being up to the new job. Not that there wasn't much to learn about how to behave in the new harness, but I had been in action in both policy and liaison before, and my previous ninth-floor experience had given me enough exposure to other areas of the job to give me an acceptable comfort level going in.

The first special assignment was to take over from Bob Drake—whose plate had just gotten fuller with his appointment as the new DDO—as NSA's Program Manager for Third Party Matters. Without getting into classified levels, that involved whatever relationships we had with most foreign governments, as well as with those U.S. departments and agencies which were also involved. Since these relationships had always embraced responsibilities throughout the Agency as well as in other U.S. government departments and agencies, there were some very complicated program elements that had to be managed. And, of course, following Bob Drake was never an easy task, God love him.

We established a TPPM steering group (it may have been in place under Bob Drake), consisting of representatives from the major NSA organizations with axes to grind, and a senior CIA member with his own ax. Meeting regularly we were able to root out problem areas and try to solve them. For the most part we succeeded, due mostly to the caliber of people on the team and their honest willingness to find answers. Jack Devine, Gene Becker, John Monroe, and Ed Fitzgerald were all members of that group at various times, all of them Class A, including at least one of the several CIA representatives.

Early on in another area of this assignment, the Agency was called upon to be a part of the first major Congressional investigation into intelligence. Most of my other Asst Dir tasks were put into second priority from late '75 until well into '76 while we were largely occupied by responding to the Church-Pike committees. Otis Pike (D-NY) chaired the House committee and Frank Church (D-Idaho) chaired the Senate. In between, other House members—never loath to get a bit of publicity (a particularly unpleasant member, Bella Abzug, made much sound and some fury, but never featured in any productive part of the hearings)—stuck their oars in whenever there appeared to be some room on the pond, and sometimes when there wasn't.

It is not that there had not been Congressional oversight, of a sort, of NSA's activities over the years since 1952. There had been but it was almost exclusively on budget issues. Traditionally it was carried out by a few senior members of each House, in behalf of the Committees of the whole. I was aware that limited interaction between NSA—usually Dr. Tordella—and the Senate (I remember Sen. Leverett Saltonstall (R-Mass) as one of the principals) regularly took place. Dr. T. did not hold back anything as far as I was aware (admittedly my awareness was of things at much lower levels in those days), nor did the Senate complain. In fact, Dr. T. had such a record and appearance of probity that Sen Saltonstall reportedly said that "If Dr. Tordella says he needs it, he needs it"; and the Senate went along. Dr. T. was as careful about spending tax money as anyone I had ever known. I don't think the Senate was ever hoodwinked by us—or the House, either.

But these '75 and '76 inquiries were from a different kettle indeed. In the aftermath of the Watergate period, serious undermining of trust between executive and legislative branches caused the Congress to go at some of us executive branch agencies with very sharp knives. As mentioned above, the Church and Pike committees took on the job of investigating the intelligence agencies. Most of the attention was focused on CIA—properly so—but NSA was subjected to public examination for the first time in its history. Senator Church forced NSA's director to testify in open session for the first time in our history.

The details, such as are of concern to my own story, are covered more fully in my monograph titled "NSA Out of the Closet", and even more extensively in Jim Hudec's article on the subject of <u>Shamrock</u>. The most immediate impact on NSA was the need to prepare for the Director's public testimony. To provide him background on the subject—since all of it had occurred prior to his watch—General Allen set up a special staff group to prepare background data for his use and for sharing with the Congressional committees. I was placed in charge of the group (of about a dozen very capable professionals). With help from us, but mostly because of his own enormous capabilities and personality, the Director successfully carried out this historic—for us—appearance on the public stage.

In the course of this exercise I was privy to the inner workings of the Senate as never before or since. Meetings with the staffs of the Church committee showed me that the substance of the investigation came in a distinct second to the interests of political partisanship. I have ever since been wary of the workings of Congress. That is not to say that committee staffs are not necessary, or that they can never provide useful insight that the Congress needs. But it does say that we must be wary . . . very wary.

And I learned another valuable lesson about how the executive branch (the Administration) and the Congress sometimes interact. Example: the explosive conflict between Sen Goldwater and SecDef

Schlesinger; details not for this memoir, but available on request from the writer . . . here I will say only that Sen Goldwater was the good guy.

One of the outcomes of this all was increased networking between various elements of the Congress and NSA and its people. While this all had both good and bad effects on us during the remainder of my career, in my experience there was more good than bad. Since this is largely about me, I will concentrate on my personal reaction for believing they were good.

The investigations of CIA and NSA by the select committees of the House and Senate whetted the appetites of other Congressional committees. House and Senate Armed Services committees and the House Appropriations committee were among the most active. One of the results was a recommendation by Appropriations to strengthen NSA's management of cryptologic activities wherever they were carried out. Similar in intent to the executive orders which led to the CSS, the Congress' initiative had the Power of the Purse behind it, and that made a great difference. I was to spend a large part of my remaining time at NSA helping to work out arrangements between us and the CIA aimed at realizing the House Committee's intent—which, of course, we agreed with.

A major part of the challenge was to make the necessary shifts and titrivations as palatable as they could be—or at least palatable enough for CIA (and some in NSA) to ingest. I am proud that we were able to make this happen. Many folks were involved. Some were for it, some against. But the major players, including Mr. Buffham, Bob Drake and myself from NSA, and several CIA seniors brought it off.

"It" was a formal agreement which spelled out a number of changes in the NSA-CIA relationship in the SIGINT world. (Note: I have since read that NSA Director Adm Bobby Inman has been given credit for this all, but I believe that his part, not unimportant to be sure, was to officiate over the end game after we had worked it out.)

A major role in making significant parts of the new NSA-CIA agreement work in its early months fell to my lot. With much help from a few seniors in CIA and NSA both, we were able to make them take root, and even show some promise of fruit to come.

One of several productive changes was a more direct relationship between NSA and its foreign counterparts. That occupied much of my remaining time at NSA, involving much travel to foreign parts, and many visits from foreign parts to us. Here again, as in so many other areas of my career and life, Betty was once more at the heart of the matter. Not only did she bear a personal burden from my trips abroad, but she was the superb hostess to the new world which came to call. I know for certain that she was an important reason for the success of our new relationships, as she certainly had been in so many previous ones. As everyone involved was careful to let me know!

The remainder of Gen. Allen's tenure as DIRNSA went by quickly. I must be forgiven for my admiration for him as a person and a boss. I make no secret of it; I believe him to be the best of the directors I served under, the very best of an outstanding lot. One of the great privileges of my career in government was to have served under him as one of his chief lieutenants.

When General Allen was called by the Air Force to his fourth star and, ultimately, to the job of Air Force Chief of Staff (see, I wasn't the only one . . .), he was replaced by a rising new star in the person of VADM Bobby Inman. Adm Inman had been for some time a fast burner in the U.S. Intelligence roster. He had served on the CNO's staff as perhaps the youngest director of naval intelligence and had gone on to be the vice director of the Defense Intelligence Agency. His credentials and his personal performance won him a deserved reputation as one of the nation's foremost intelligence officers. In my own view he is one of the top intelligence analysts in our country's history.

Interestingly enough, in the final weeks of Gen. Allen's time as Director, he had sent me as his substitute on a group of intelligence community seniors charged with reviewing DOD policy on an ongoing high-level review of—surprise—intelligence organization. Admiral Inman, who was the leading rumored nominee to become the new Director, NSA, was the DIA-JCS J2 representative on that group. I have written elsewhere of the surprising encounter we had at one of the group's meetings. (It was a brief conversation during a break, at which Adm. Inman told me that he had heard I was a member of a rump-group at NSA trying to bring about a civilian Director. I told him that I certainly was not.) While I, naively as it was to turn out, dismissed it as just one of those sidebars, it must have had a more lasting effect on him.

Nonetheless, I was continued in my job as the assistant director for policy and liaison during Adm. Inman's reign at NSA, until my retirement in 1980. We developed a good working relationship and an excellent personal affinity. He and wife Nancy were fun to be with, and we were pleased to be included in their circle of friends as well as senior partners.

But these final two years with NSA were bittersweet. More sweet than bitter, but bittersweet nonetheless. The sweetness derived from being able to continue working at a meaningful job in a meaningful element of our national security structure. Each day was a challenge, bringing its problems and opportunities from the worldwide system we helped manage, its satisfactions at things which worked, and its frustrations at things which didn't. Above it all there was a constant awareness that what we were about was really important, and that what we were contributing might make a difference. We used to sum it up by saying we "had a seat at the table"—a very significant table indeed.

And the bitter? Very hard to come to grips with, and even harder to explain. At first there was nothing tangible. There was no immediate reorganization, no basic changes to what the agency did or how it went about doing it. There were some variances in the operations of the Director's immediate staff, but nothing really more or less than was to be expected from any new Chief.

The new Director was an extraordinary player. He grasped the internal details of the business with amazing speed. He worked the Congress and the intelligence community as well or better than any of his predecessors, establishing or fostering relationships important to our standing within government. His interests were all encompassing and his intellect was enormous, enabling him to take on and store the information on plans, programs, budgets, organization, etc. in the most minute detail. In short, he was a most impressive fellow.

The real business of the Agency went on normally, performed as usual by its analysts, linguists, engineers, mathematicians and support areas, and as usual unaffected by peripheral matters, such as a change of command on the ninth floor. The rest of us continued to deal with our part in helping them in their critically important work.

Among other things, we gave much attention to programs we had designed to help us interact with our customer base; and we were newly involved in responding to (and minimizing distraction from) the oversight functions of the Congress. A fair share of my day was claimed by these concerns.

Additionally, for the first time in my experience, I became involved in responding to White House interest in our routine technological review for DOD of proposed high-technology exports. For whatever reasons, we were asked to re-do our examinations on pending export cases. We did, and when our analysts came up with the same negative responses, we passed this as our Agency position back to the White House staff. In answer to repeated pressure to re-review, I finally said in effect that NSA could understand that there might be political reasons which would cause them to override our security concerns, but that we could not take that burden from them by lowering our own technological barriers. They went away on this case—my suspect memory is that the export was approved but with significant modification—but they would be back again.

These last years were, however, punctuated by a number of jarring (for me) policy issues. In retrospect, they involved arguably understandable changes between previous practices and new ideas from a new and different Director. And yet . . .

When the Director surfaced to his Senior Management Council a proposal to get closer to the moguls of the press by "sharing" selected sensitive data—the idea being to get them to hold off publishing "unknowingly" damaging reports—I was taken by surprise. He had not given my policy office any hint of this new direction. I was one of only two of his senior council members to voice objection. He then announced at that same meeting that he had already begun this new policy, and the issue became moot. Subsequent experience has shown the policy (even to Adm. Inman, I believe) to have not been worth its costs. But for me it was a Pyrrhic victory. I would not have chosen to oppose him, or any director, in such a forum, without prior discussion.

At about this time the (Carter) administration had introduced changes to the Civil Service in an effort to get around the freeze on the highest pay (supergrade) levels. A Senior Executive Service was created; it provided among other things for "performance" cash bonuses which would not count against frozen salary levels. The Agency was considering buying into an amended version of this program, tailored to meet our special security requirements. It was ultimately adopted against minority opposition (mine).

Again, I made no secret of my opposition to performance bonuses to senior officials. I argued that our compensation should be based on the level of responsibility/difficulty of the position—not superior performance, which should be a given. And that the bonus idea was a sham to avoid facing the real issue, which was the inability to pay senior folks what they were worth.

While my objection—based, as usual, on high-minded principle—turned out to be sound, it didn't matter. President Reagan's revolutionary pay raises for executives (and Congress) later wiped out the freezes anyway; but the bonuses, and the expensive system that houses them, have continued long after their reason for existence has vanished.

What was the most difficult for me to accept was the growing use by the Director of skip-echelon management. Especially the fact that MY echelon was being skipped, although it was clear that I was not alone in this feeling. The Admiral was especially good at detail, and remembering it, and being able to concentrate on any number of relatively minor matters. Coupled with his propensity to communicate directly with talent at many levels within the Agency, he was able to address detailed program and people issues with working levels, without the slower process of using existing organizational structure. It allowed him to operate at his usual warp speed, but in the long term it undermined those who worked for him in the chain of command.

Finally, there was the delayed revamping of the organization itself. The Director had decided to recombine Agency-level Policy and Planning functions into one Deputy Directorate. Although I was not consulted on the move, I thought it was a good one (it had been the mode under earlier Directors) and said so to Bob Drake –Buffham's replacement as Deputy Director. He had been tasked by the Director to tell me. Drake also said that the intent was to fill this new job with someone who would be slated to go on to be the Director of Operations. And that person was not going to be me.

Fair enough, I said. And where do I go, I said. And that's where the pill became bitter. The job they had in mind for me was just not acceptable to me: Dep. Asst. Director for Plans and Resources—the "money plus planning" job, soon to become the money minus planning job—with the prospect of replacing the current ADPR in the near future. It was definitely not a move onward. And rather than to haggle about it, or to become part of the problem rather than the solution, I decided on the spot that I should retire. Drake then told me that he, too, had decided to retire, and I began to see a pattern.

The Director subsequently offered a number of alternative positions, some of them jobs I had filled before—but not under him, the Director said—and none with a seat "at the table". Finally, in what I believed to be an honest attempt to keep me on board, the Admiral suggested the position of SUSLO, our senior rep to the UK. While this was the job I had always hoped to get one day, our family situation at that time would not permit it. And besides, I believed that I had passed the point of no return.

So it was that at the end of February 1980 I finished a most rewarding career with the National Security Agency.

Post-Script: I should not have retired when I did. I was not ready for retirement, and I made the move for the wrong reasons. Probably the "wrongest" of them was that I let my Irish overrule my judgment. I had more to give, but I was too proud, and for once, too impatient to wait for another day to do it. But, from another perspective it may well have worked out for the better. I'll write about why in the post-retirement years sketches.

Author being presented with the Exceptional Civilian Service
Award by NSA Director Lt. Gen. Allen—1975

Harney family with Gen.
Allen and Mr. Buffham at the
Exceptional Civilian Service
Award ceremony—1975

Author at his NSA retirement
celebration—1980

LIFE AFTER NSA

I retired from NSA on the last day of February 1980. I will attempt to pick up the narrative after five years or so of writing about other things. The passage of more than 25 years since this phase of my story begins will test—and soften—my recollections of post retirement doings.

As I wrote in the last chapter, my departure from NSA was not without trauma. It was also far from the smartest thing I have done. I left in a fit of Irish pique at having been sidelined (as I believed at the time, and still do) by the then-Director. While I recognized and accepted his right to do so, and even agreed (erroneously as it turned out) with his stated motive, I could not swallow being removed from the First Team, and so I left. Events show that I probably could have survived the setback—and the bad taste in my mouth—far less dramatically.

At any rate, I retired. It was not only a bad thing for me personally, but it was worse for Betty. She was already overburdened by her duties as a grandmother of twins and being a principal support for their mother (who was preparing to add to the family), but she was in the process of settling in her own parents who had come to live under her care. Enter a husband who felt cut adrift from his other life, and the weight on her shoulders would have been intolerable to most of the best of the rest. But not to her.

I had not made plans for retirement, because I had not planned to retire. But I had determined that I would not be one of those (very few, at that time, but growing) who chose to build on their NSA careers by securing jobs with related private industry. Not that the practice was widespread or necessarily evil in any real sense, but I had determined that it was not for me. Kind of like the impractical high-mindedness that had suffused me after graduating from college. And just about as dumb.

I was left with the non-productive choice of whether to play golf or to spend time on equally unremunerative pro bono tasks. When a chronic back problem reduced my golfing time substantially, I was even less occupied. After about two years of this—I can't believe I let it last that long—Betty let me know that ALL of us, she and I, the children, and her aging parents—would be better off if I could only find something to do which would occupy me elsewhere.

Being not a complete dumbbell, I modified my holier-than-thou attitude about industry and took a job with the Watkins-Johnson electronics company. But with the understanding that I was not to be involved in anything connected with selling the company's wares to NSA. The Company and I maintained that disconnect throughout my seven-year stay.

The immediate cause for my selecting W-J was a chance meeting at that time with Ron Bell, a sometime acquaintance during his time at NSA. The job I was offered in the process of being hired was to establish a European headquarters for W-J and to stimulate (actually, to revive) interest in W-J systems. Since W-J had just begun to be interested itself in "systems", this was a larger task than I could appreciate at the time. For a number of reasons, this pre-hire intent was not to be realized during my time with them, nor thereafter.

The short version is: after I looked at the company's position, I did not believe that establishing such a headquarters—I was given the choice of Brussels, London, or Bonn—was warranted. I believed that I could do what I perceived as "my job" from the central location offered by the Washington area—roughly equidistant from the W-J home office in California and the European market—without the expense to the Company, or the personal dislocation for me and mine involved in the "overseas headquarters" plan. The Company decided to agree, and I set out to test whether we were correct.

At any rate, the Company hired me (for $20K per year less than had been advertised to me) and I began part two of my working career. It was a very interesting, quite illuminating, but in the end disappointing seven-plus years. In brief, I was too late for what the Company had had in mind, and W-J was not capable of adjusting its sights. This and several other not totally unrelated missteps hastened its premature and, I believe, unnecessary demise. But I had, as said, a quite interesting ride while it was still alive.

I spent most of my time and energy working on European International business, concentrating on requirements and business development in Germany and Scandinavia. As a first step, I made the rounds of W-J's existing business structure in Europe. Since almost all of that was sales related, I accompanied the Manager of International Sales to "major" W-J international centers in Bonn, Munich, Rome, Windsor (U.K.), and minor reps in Athens. (There were related others in Israel and various reps in Scandinavia, but they were not to be part of my beat.)

This was to be the first of many overseas trips for the Company. They placed additional stress on home and family, as my many travels for NSA had done. The down-side of my "getting out of being underfoot" in Betty's chock-full household is obvious. The children had, it's true, moved out to their own digs, but except for John they were far from absent. Betty's advanced grandmothering skills were in constant use and her care-giving for her parents in constant demand. Added duties in "business" entertaining (which she was great at) occupied her remaining "free" time.

A large part of my activities involved showcasing of W-J "systems" at overseas locations (with invaluable help from the local Bonn office, especially from Gene Kitzmiller). Most of them (the systems) were under development themselves, and inconveniently chose to display all their "bugs" while they were supposed to be demonstrating their value. Nonetheless, W-J's reputation (built by its superior "boxes") served to maintain our access to their markets despite all-too-frequent systems failures to perform adequately. We remained in contention for sizable contracts, but the trend was clearly ominous. And all this was happening at a time of lowered defense spending in that market and growing indigenous competition.

At about the year two marker, a new CEI/Gaithersburg VP chose to put me to work closer to home (in addition to lingering overseas tasks) and I assumed responsibilities for overseeing Personnel, Contracting, Plant Operations and associated areas, all of which I had assiduously avoided throughout my NSA career. Could have been a disaster if either I or the hands-on managers had paid much attention to the Org Chart!

The frosting on my management cake, however, was still to come. I was appointed Manager of Advanced Development for the CEI Div. In reality, the job was designed to justify the funds we were spending and hoping to attract more of for our IR&D (Internal Research and Development) efforts. That meant, the Division's future. But within a few years, the Division was to have no future . . . I steadfastly maintain that I did nothing to cause that to happen, nor could I have done anything to forestall it. It was foreordained by Company policies which encouraged (actually required) its individual divisions to compete with each other as if they were independent companies, not merely cost-and-profit centers. In a few instances that worked to the Company's benefit; in more than one, it was a disaster. And nowhere did it make less sense than in the IR&D programs, where the need to consolidate technologic research funding and coordinate research projects should have been self-evident.

As one result, the CEI Div I worked for was merged into, and subordinated to, a competing division. While this had little to do with my management skills—in fact I really enjoyed and feel I was good at that part of the challenge I was charged with—it effectively ended my useful employment with W-J. Nevertheless, my mind still boggles at the picture of me, the last guy to get the electric bell circuit to work in our 7th grade shop class, in nominal charge of the efforts of a bunch of really bright young graduate electronics engineers to move our company from the analog to the digital world! And they say that the U.S. Federal Government is poorly managed!

I finished my days at W-J in an unsuccessful attempt to get the Company to improve its ability to UNDERSTAND, and move to cope with, the rapidly advancing target technologies its major customers were facing. It was hard to do this within the limits I had set for myself at the outset, but without too much stretching of them I undertook this self-imposed task. No matter; it was too little, too late, and too hard for the Company to digest. It was also too bad, because W-J might have contributed more to its customers in their tough, tough roads ahead.

And that—except for a heart attack, thousands of air miles, and a graduate-level course in what defense-related industry in a stock market driven world looked like—was that!

Oh, yes . . . there was also the money. I was able to supplement substantially my U.S Government retirement checks, even though I was more of a bargain than I knew at the time of hire. Ignorant as I was of how the electronics job market worked—stock options and all that stuff—I came cheaply. Although in a company that based its compensations directly on sales, I must admit that I didn't do all that poorly for a guy who refused to be part of direct sales to its major customers. Nevertheless, I learned fairly soon that I had jumped into the job market much too quickly and without the required examination of relevant alternatives. But as the saying goes, "Vee get too zoon oldt, und too late schmart . . ."

As a result of the W-J job, we were able to buy a weekend place on Rehoboth Bay, which the family got some pleasure from and which I could use on occasion to entertain business folk. (As Betty would certainly agree, I was too quick to sell it after re-retiring from W-J.) And W-J made it possible for Betty and daughter Kathy to revisit with me some of our Germany past.

I retired from W-J in 1989, just as I was turning age 65. I cannot leave this segment of my story without emphasizing once again how important and impressive wife Betty was, how much she helped my efforts directly and indirectly, and how she managed to weather her Dad's death and her mother's increasing dependence. And how she brought me through my heart episode so well.

My experience with W-J's European market and my earlier extensive involvement with European government interests, capabilities, and potential value to cooperation with U.S. in electronic matters—and to be honest, my own desires to remain involved AND BUSY—led me to forming my own consulting firm "Europe and U.S. (EURUS)". Offering value to U.S. firms which sought involvement with and mutual benefit from coordinated efforts, we were (I was) able to develop and add to the process. Not being versed in business, the company had limited success, substantially because the European market was understandably more involved in developing its own capabilities than in seeking the kind of cooperative development at the levels we had in mind. Accordingly, the business success of EURUS was fleeting, and minor.

- Never mind . . . in my work at W-J I had become familiar with advances in computer technology to the point where I had begun to recognize applications in other than W-J applications. And I turned my attention to them. Which led in part to some interesting ideas which might have, but did not enrich us.

As a sideline to EURUS, I began to work with an old friend and colleague from NSA, Bill Cox, who was at the time deeply involved in the Washington Redskins Alumni Association. Bill, an All-American quarterback from Duke, had been drafted by the 'Skins as a potential replacement for quarterback Sammy Baugh. After a brief career in the NFL, where he played with, not in place of, Sammy, he had been "drafted" by the NSA where he served to retirement. And then became active in the Redskins alumni, where he served as a kind of Executive Assistant to the President.

Bill asked my help in working on the details of some way for the Redskins Alumni to detach themselves from the NFL Alumni Association. Which I did and they did. In the process I also became involved in their alumni charitable activities, mostly those involving fund-raising and disbursing, themselves largely funded from their annual Spring Golf Tournament.

As an active associate of their Alumni, I had some access to the Redskins organization, of the Joe Gibbs era. This included a tour of their training area, centered on their filming practices which I, applying my newly-won appreciation of the miracle of modern data processing, judged to be archaic to obsolescent. With my EURUS hat on, I developed the rudiments of a computer-driven system for digital photographing, storing, and retrieving game and practice sessions. It would have replaced the archaic system of individual film canisters, their storage, and their lending out to the various coaches and players who wished to study them.

It would have been a huge jump forward into the digital world. While it would have required a serious investment by management, once developed, even using that day's technology it would inevitably have brought enormous returns on its own (to our knowledge no other franchise had it, or was working on it) and from related use during games and in sharing as required by the NFL. But management did not respond—an upsetting probability is that management never knew about it, since the team official we talked to was the one who ran their current system and was invested in its survival. At any rate, this was one of several business opportunities I had, any one of which could have resulted in someone else's writing about my part in them.

While this was (or was not) going on, I began to write my memoir, part of which you may be reading now, but in between I wrote down my thoughts of what was happening in and to our country, elsewhere in the world, and how we should or should not be reacting. Wars, political crises, religious strife and other political affairs. Most of my thoughts I attempted to share through copious letters to various Editors, and in essays on various political and social developments in the world, which I now had more time to think about. These I have been assembling and with the help of my children hope to see published in one form or another.

I had not, nor do I ever hope to, cut the ties with NSA and its people and institutions. In the process of "not cutting ties" I accepted a position on the Board of The NSA Phoenix Society, and later on the Board of the Association of Former Intelligence Officers (AFIO). These kept me reasonably busy, and then came Florida. To get away from the unpleasantness of the Maryland/DC winters, Betty and I chose to spend much of our winter months in rented quarters on Florida's West Coast.

While we enjoyed the weather (and I got to play much golf—of which I will write some in future pages) we also got to play socially with a group of pleasant rebels from Georgia, by whom we were accepted as Yankee expatriates. In the excess time of our winter stays, Betty and I patronized the local libraries, and learned things we had not had time for in our more productive years. Some of what I learned from the Largo Library is reflected in my amateur essays on Religion and more in a book to be published as Part Two of my Memoir.